How to Restore
Automotive Trim
and Hardware

By John Gunnell

motorbooks

Dedication

Dedicated to my father, Albert A. Gunnell, who passed while this book was in progress.
Dad and I spent many days tinkering with his cars and with my first car
back in the mid-1960s. More important, he put ideas in my head
that steered me toward a writing career.

First published in 2009 by Motorbooks, an imprint of MBI Publishing Company, 400 First Avenue North, Suite 300, Minneapolis, MN 55401 USA

Motorbooks titles are also available at discounts in bulk quantity for industrial or sales-promotional use. For details write to Special Sales Manager at MBI Publishing Company, 400 First Avenue North, Suite 300, Minneapolis, MN 55401 USA.

To find out more about our books, join us online at www.motorbooks.com.

ISBN-00: 978-0-7603-3531-4

Library of Congress Cataloging-in-Publication Data

Gunnell, John, 1947–
  How to restore automotive trim and hardware / John Gunnell.
      p. cm.
  Includes bibliographical references.
  ISBN 978-0-7603-3531-4 (pbk. : alk. paper)
  1. Automobiles—Bodies—Parts—Maintenance and repair.
  2. Automobiles—Conservation and restoration. I. Title.
  TL255.G85 2009
  629.28'72—dc22
                              2009005002

Editor: Chris Endres
Designer: Danielle Smith

Printed in Singapore

On the cover: 1958 Pontiac Bonneville Tri-Power.
Dennis Adler/AutoStockHause

About the author
John Gunnell grew up in Staten Island, New York, and attended Brooklyn Technical High School. He got sidetracked from his goal of becoming an industrial designer and wound up with a degree in fine arts. In 1978, he had the opportunity to join the staff of *Old Cars Weekly* in Iola, Wisconsin. He worked there for 30 years and was involved in all aspects of the old-car hobby. He was editor of *Old Cars Price Guide*, publisher of *Old Cars Weekly*, and team leader for the company's automotive books department. "Gunner," as he is known to many people, currently contributes to more than 25 magazines in the vintage car, motorcycle, and airplane fields. John lives in Iola where he tries hard to keep ten cars and trucks and three motorcycles functioning at all times.

Contents

Introduction

This book started out as *How to Restore Metal Auto Trim* by Jeff Lilly. Jeff is a professional restorer in San Antonio, Texas, and his book was a professional-level guide to this topic. It is the *standard* reference work for anyone who wants to repair bright metal trim on their collector vehicles. The Eastwood Company, which sells the specialty tools and supplies needed to do this work, includes Jeff's book in its kit of buffing aids.

When Jeff said he was not interested in doing a revised and expanded trim restoration book, MBI asked me to try. Truthfully, I thought it would be easy to redo an existing book and update it with color photos. I thought I could just visit a shop that does stainless-steel buffing, take a few photos, and bingo! But things didn't quite go that way.

Unlike Jeff, I do not pay my bills by restoring cars. I'm a professional writer, and I have 30 years of experience in the old-car hobby. Yes, I have a few vehicles (11) that I tinker with. Yes, I have an Eastwood buffer and supply of rouges that I use occasionally. You might say that I know "just enough to get me in trouble" about buffing. But, I also know lots of restorers. So, I decided to do a different kind of book relying on my car-collecting communications skills and the buffing knowledge of experts I've met over 30 years from all parts of the country.

As I started working on the book with MBI editor Peter Schletty, I found out that MBI wanted me to write about a broader range of skills than covered in Jeff Lilly's classic metal buffing guide. The hobby had changed a bit, and MBI was being asked for information on newer products and about restoring cars with plastic trim. Hobbyists restoring muscle cars wanted to know about chroming plastic parts. Younger restorers wanted to learn how they could redo the carbon fiber trim on their "new millennium" cars.

I told Peter Schletty that a lot of these restoration skills are not appropriate for home shops, so we made the Appendix much larger to list all the vendors who can help. We also added a photo essay on restoration hardware to the ending chapter of the book to cover this important subject. Hardware suppliers are also listed in the Appendix.

Editor Chris Endres took over the project in midstream to "light a fire under" the lazy author and to guide the book to completion. Chris made the always-challenging wrap-up of a yearlong project simple and easy.

What we wound up with is a great deal of expert advice gathered from professionals throughout the country that was organized for you by a home restorer who knows a bit about communications and compiling books. We hope—in other words—that you'll find good information that's easy to read.

This, of course, is different from the do-it-every-day, hands-on advice that Jeff Lilly packed into *How to Restore Auto Trim*. And if I were interested in learning how to restore the trim on one of my own cars, trucks, and motorcycles, I would want *both* of these books on the D-I-Y bookshelf in my home restoration shop.

John Gunnell

Acknowledgments

The restorers and other people who helped me put this book together are all mentioned in the text. Their contact information will be found in the Appendix. The other people and companies listed in the Appendix are reliable advertisers in *Old Cars Weekly* and other hobby publications. I am not going to try to reacknowledge all these professionals here. Other people who helped me with advice and inspiration were Colin Bruce, Chester L. Krause, John Marks, Zack Miller, "Cowboy" Bob Norris, Dennis Peterson, Jim Rugowski, Angelo Van Bogart, and Jim Wagner of Zero-to-60 Garage. My son Jesse Gunnell supplied a number of his great photos and sometimes served as my "hand model" for shop photos.

Photos in this book were taken at the Atlantic City Classic Car Auction & Swap Meet, the Cycle World Trade Show in Indianapolis, the vintage race venues at Road America in Elkhart Lake, Wisconsin, the S & S Cycle 50th Anniversary Celebration in La Crosse, Wisconsin, Bloomington Gold, the Iola Old Car Show, the Appleton Auto Show, the Botham Winery Vintage Festival, the Masterpiece of Style & Speed, the Antique Motorcycle Club of America (Blackhawk Chapter) National Meet in Davenport, Iowa, and the Greenfield Village Old Car Festival. Without these events and many others, there would be no old-vehicle hobby.

Chapter 1
Bright Metal Auto Trim

HISTORY OF METAL AUTO TRIM

"Give them something to look at," General Motors designer Bill Mitchell once said about car buyers. "You throw a billiard ball to a guy and he puts it down, but (not) a baseball. He'll keep playing with it (because of) the stitches."[1]

For years, bright metal auto trim added "stitches" to car designs. This "tinsel" is an intricate part of collectible vehicles and must be restored if you want a factory-new look. You do not have to own a '58 Buick, '58 Olds, or '59 Caddy (three of history's "chromiest" cars) to be interested in bright metal auto trim restoration.

Bright metal trim was used from the start. The Crestline *Packard* book (MBI 1996) shows William Doud Packard driving an 1899 runabout with kerosene head and side lamps and a decorative dashboard rail. The lamps had brass highlights and the rail was made of brass.[2]

By 1904, Packard acquired the "tombstone" brass radiator. Brass "drum" headlights flanked it. Radiator mascots brightened up cars and added individuality. And the use of metal trim grew. Bright touches soon included brass "loop" door handles, running board boxes with shiny hinges, and aluminum running board trim strips. Hubcaps, windshield stanchions, and steering wheel masts were made of polished brass.

In the 1920s, models like sport touring cars featured running board step plates. Bright-finished vertical rails on the rear kept touring trunks from slamming into the sheet metal. By this time, headlight tie bars were used. Bumpers arrived and body styles with bright landau irons became a fashion rage.

History books indicate that the use of bright metal moldings to accentuate "feature lines" of cars started in the

The '58 Buick was one of the most trim-laden American cars ever built. Legend has it that Chrysler's all-new 1957 "Forward Look" shocked him so much that General Motors design chief Harley Earl ordered 100 pounds of chrome added to his cars.

Bright metal trim was used from the early days of the auto industry. This 1909 Economy Model G Touring has brass headlights and running lamps, brass hubcaps, a brass bulb horn, and a brass acetylene tank.

1920s. Custom coachbuilders applied them before factories did. In the 1930s, the use of bright metal trim increased. Even low-priced cars had chrome-plated hood doors and chrome "surrounds" for side-mounted tires.

By the late 1930s, many cars had three chrome grilles—one in front and one in each fender catwalk—plus grilles decorating the hood sides, shiny belt moldings, chrome window moldings, large "pie plate" hubcaps, wheel trim rings, and massive bumpers with chrome guards.

By the 1940s, American cars were "chrome boats." Chrome-plated strips and louvers decorated the front, rear, and sides to accentuate length and width. Cadillacs, Chevrolets, and Packards carried fender "speed bars." Accessories like chrome-badged fender skirts, stainless-steel gravel shields, and windshield spotlights were popular. In 1943, designer Raymond Loewy criticized the appearance of American cars as "too bulky and loaded with chromium spinach and schmaltz."[3]

By the 1950s, GM designer Harley Earl moved from using chrome as a finishing touch to making it a part of car design. He developed chrome treatments like the sweep-spear, the blitz line, the continuous drip molding, and the Tiffany grille. The industry followed, until 1957, when Chrysler's Virgil Exner launched the "Forward Look." Suddenly, it was tomorrow. Earl reacted by ordering that hundreds of pounds of chrome be attached to '58 Buicks and Oldsmobiles to freshen their looks. From the 1960s on, the use of bright metal trim declined. "Form follows function" was the creed of younger designers.

DIFFERENT METALS USED FOR AUTO TRIM

Restorers will find themselves dealing with different metals when restoring trim. Early "brass era" cars used brass trim. By 1912, German silver was used. Nickel plating arrived in the teens. Chrome-plated parts came later. Stainless steel grew popular. Aluminum, copper, zinc, and magnesium are other metals restorers must deal with.

It's important to know the properties of a metal. They determine its use on a car and the proper way to restore it. The tools, products, and skills needed to restore different metals vary. Knowing the properties helps determine what it takes to make it look new again.

Brass

A brass radiator Model T looks fancier than a steel radiator T. Brass is a copper-zinc alloy. The proportions can be tweaked to create over 15 different types of brass. Brass is a decorative metal with a shiny, muted yellow appearance. It also has acoustic properties and low friction, making it useful for parts like locks and bells. Brass doesn't tarnish easily. It is malleable and melts at relatively low heat. Its flow characteristics make it easy to cast. It is not magnetic. Brass is lacquered to prevent it from tarnishing. Unlacquered brass weathers well and looks better than brass with deteriorated lacquer. Brass must be polished to maintain a bright finish. Polished brass is goldlike. It grows reddish when exposed to the elements.

German silver

In 1913, Oakland used a "rounded V-shaped radiator with German silver finish." German silver is a type of nickel silver—a copper-nickel-zinc alloy. In 1770, the Suhl Metalworks in Germany produced this alloy. Later, the Berndorf Company perfected it as Alpacca. German silver became a popular substrate after electroplating was developed in the 1840s. It was strong and had a bright, silvery appearance. Unplated German silver was used in making cutlery. German silver is shiny, corrosion resistant (without lacquer finish), and machineable. It has high electrical resistance.

Nickel

Nickel plating is found on many classic cars. Nickel is a silvery-white metal that takes on a high polish. It is hard and ductile. Nickel is very reactive but is slow to react in air at normal temperatures and pressures. It is magnetic. Due to its permanence in air and resistance to rusting, it is used for plating. Nickel is found in stainless steel, magnets, coins, and special alloys. Nickel alloy is used in nickel steel, cast iron, brass, and bronze, and in alloys with copper, chromium,

By the 1940s, American cars were "chrome boats." Chrome-plated strips and louvers decorated the front, rear, and sides to accentuate length and width. This '47 Chevrolet has also had a lot of accessory trim pieces added to it.

This 1920s Oakland Sport Touring car features running board moldings and step plates. The nickel-plated radiator and headlights add other bright touches, as do the bumpers, door handles, hubcaps, and plated windshield frame.

Introduced a year before this '36 Pontiac was made, the company's Silver Streak stainless-steel hood moldings became a brand trademark for over two decades. Restorers today want their Silver Streaks to look perfect.

Starting in the late 1950s and continuing into the early 1960s, stamped aluminum grilles became popular. The aluminum grille on this '63 Dodge is made of rust-resistant metal, but it has other aging issues that restorers must deal with.

aluminum, lead, cobalt, silver, and gold. Nickel has been used as a substitute for silver in decorative applications. Nickel-plated parts have a different look than chrome-plated parts. Restorers must be aware of this to ensure that a 1930s car is properly restored.

Stainless steel

"Stainless" is an important auto trim metal. By definition, any iron-carbon alloy with over 11.5 percent chromium by weight is stainless. These metals do not stain or rust as easily as regular steel. The chromium content forms a thin *passivation* layer that lets the base metal shine through but protects it against moisture and air. After milling, stainless is sold in sheet, plate, bar, wire, and tube form. There are over 150 grades. Carbon stainless steel is very hard and strong. Nickel stainless steel is nonmagnetic and less brittle at low temperatures. Martenistic stainless steel is harder, stronger, tougher, more machineable, and more brittle. Stainless can be difficult to bend and shape. It is used to make thin trim moldings because the thinner it is, the easier to shape.

Chrome

Chromium is a steel gray hard metal that can be polished to a shiny appearance. It is malleable and has a high melting point. When *passivated* by oxygen, chromium forms a thin, transparent, protective oxide layer that resists the air and moisture that causes rust. In automotive applications, a super thin layer of chrome is electroplated onto a substrate of nickel that's first been copper-plated. The substrates are also acid etched. High-quality chrome plating will result in a smooth chrome deposit of uniform thickness that is free of pits, pinholes, and dull-looking areas. Since special equipment is necessary to do chrome plating, this is not a job the hobbyist can tackle at home. Knowing what talents to look for in a plater is important, though.

Aluminum

Used in cars since the earliest days of the industry, aluminum is a soft, lightweight metal. Aluminum can range in appearance from dull gray to silvery, depending on how smooth it is. It is nonmagnetic and won't create sparks when friction is applied. In auto trim applications, it saves weight. Aluminum is easy to shape due to its high ductibility. It can be readily extruded, machined, and cast. It is extremely corrosion resistant. Mirror-finished aluminum has a very high level of reflectance. It conducts heat and electricity well. Though low in tensile strength, aluminum can be tempered to make it strong. Aluminum car parts damage easily and can be difficult or impossible to restore. This makes certain trim parts rare and hard to replace, unless they are reproduced.

Restorers must deal with different metals. Early "brass era" cars like this 1901 Curved Dash Olds had brass trim. German silver, nickel, chrome, stainless, aluminum, copper, zinc, and magnesium are other metals restorers encounter.

Nickel plating is found on many classic car parts like this 1927 Pontiac hood mascot made of cheap pot metal. Nickel is a silvery-white metal that takes on a high polish, and it really increased the eye appeal of such ornaments.

Stainless steel is an important auto trim metal. It has a high percentage of chrome in it and does not stain or rust as easily as regular steel. It is the perfect metal to use for making parts like these '47 Chevy "speedline" moldings.

Pot metal

Almost a "dirty word" among car restorers, pot metal ("monkey metal") is known for pitting, bending, twisting, and breaking. Most pot metal parts are made from zinc castings that create air bubbles and allow zinc oxide to weaken the metal. Many elements in pot metal suffer internal corrosion that causes chrome plating to lift and peel off the part. Once it seemed impossible to restore pot metal. Welding or brazing will not work due to zinc's low melting point. However, platers have developed techniques to repair some pot metal parts.

Copper, bronze, zinc, titanium, magnesium, and other metals

Other metals are used less frequently in auto trim applications. True magnesium wheels on a vintage racing car could be considered a "trim" item, and you might run across exterior hinges made from zinc castings. Such parts can be restored by polishing or buffing. Eastwood sells paints that reproduce the looks of metal parts.

DIFFERENT FINISHES OF METAL TRIM

Restorers use different methods to finish trim parts. They can change surface finishes by sanding, polishing, and buffing.

The white anodized "house siding" insert on the rear fender of the '57 Chevy Bel Air is an "applied" finish. Reproductions of the '57 Bel Air insert are available, but replacing a similar insert on a Mercury or De Soto may require custom fabrication.

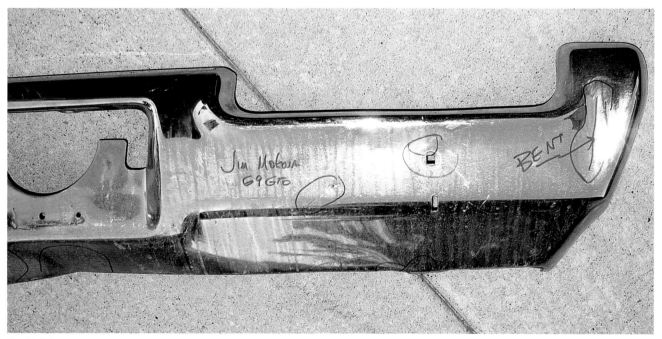

This '69 GTO bumper is marked to let the bumper shop know the owner's name and the specific areas of damage the shop is being asked to repair. Most shops accepting parts for repair also engrave the owner's name on the back of the part.

Used in cars since the early days, aluminum—like the silvery side trim on this Olds Starfire convertible—is a soft, lightweight metal. It can range in appearance from dull gray to the way it looks here, depending on its smoothness.

A restorer may want to replicate the engine-turned pattern of a vintage dashboard, the wood graining on a garnish molding, the shiny mirror finish on a chrome molding, or the satin finish on a lower grille. The three types of finishes that can be applied to metal include plating, painting, and silk screening.

With custom-polishing techniques, many variations are possible. By using different tools, abrasives, polishes, and rouges, it is possible to change the surface finish of a metal part from smooth and shiny to rough and dull.

Plating

By using chemical reactions, metal parts can be coated with substances to fight corrosion, enhance their appearance, and make them more durable. Anodizing plates aluminum with a durable decorative coating are offered in many colors. A black oxide finish can be plated on steel and ferrous metals. Chromate plating is done on aluminum substrates. Chrome plating is done on a copper over steel substrate. Other plating includes copper, gold, electroless nickel, nickel, passivate (on stainless steel), silver, tin, and zinc.

Painting

Paint puts an excellent finish on metal trim parts that were originally painted. Some builders of hot rods and custom cars do a great job of using paint to cover parts originally plated. The advantages of paint include excellent corrosion resistance and a good appearance at low cost.

Designed to minimize air pollution, powder coating is gaining wide use. Solvent-based paints suspend the pigmentation in a liquid while it is being applied. As the solvent evaporates, it leaves a film of paint. Powder coating takes advantage of static electricity to make the fine, dry powder of paint pigments cling to a part. Heat then liquefies the powder to form a film. As the part cools, the paint returns to a solid.

Screen Printing

Silk screening is used to put graphics on metal. Using a wiping paddle, an operator presses ink through a fine screen mesh to apply it to the piece. The screen mesh is stretched tightly around a frame that is lined up with the work piece. To put the ink where it belongs, the screen mesh is sealed

This '29 Pontiac hood ornament and radiator shell have been restored with high-quality chrome plating. Good "rechroming" results in a smooth chrome deposit of uniform thickness that is free of pits, pinholes, and dull-looking areas.

with a photoresist. A high contrast master art film layout is used to expose the photoresist, which is then removed by rinsing. Most of the screen mesh remains sealed after exposure. Only the desired graphics are open to pass the ink to the work piece.

Custom Polished Finishes

Different custom polishing operations can alter the finish of metal trim parts. Aluminum, stainless steel, and exotic alloys can be custom polished. Polishing with approximately 100-grit abrasives creates a semifinal finish. A general purpose, bright polished finish can be accomplished with abrasives having a particle size of 120–150 mesh, following an initial grinding with coarse abrasives. A nondirectional satin finish can be achieved by using 80–150-grit with no grain direction. Brushing the finish sheet, using a medium of abrasive and oil, produces a dull satin finish with low reflectivity. Buffing a surface that has first been finely brushed, avoiding removal of the grit lines during final buffing, can produce a highly reflective finish.

A mirror surface is the highest reflective finish. Polishing with successively finer abrasives, then buffing with a very fine buffing compound or rouge will produce it. The surface must be free of grit lines from preliminary buffing. In a variation of this technique, the trim material is finished with an orbital sander using 180–240-grit. However the sheet is viewed, there is no pattern or grain.

Stainless Steel Finishes

There are companies that can apply standard mill finishes to flat rolled stainless steel. This can be rolled onto the steel or it can be created with mechanical abrasives. In certain cases, stainless steel with a certain finish applied to it might be handy for fabricating restoration parts to replicate originals. The standard mill surface finishes are laid down in Specifications (BS 1449, Part 4, and the Committee of Stainless Steel Producers, American Iron & Steel Institute).

1. Hot rolled, annealed, thicker plates
2. Hot rolled, annealed, and passivated

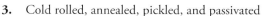

3. Cold rolled, annealed, pickled, and passivated
4. Cold rolled, annealed, pickled, and passivated with additional roller polishing
5. Bright annealed – same as No. 4, but highly polished rollers are used
6. Coarse abrasive finish applied mechanically
7. Brushed finish
8. Satin finish
9. Matte finish
10. Reflective finish
11. Mirror finish
12. Bead blast finish

IDENTIFYING MISSING TRIM

Missing trim cannot be replaced unless the restorer knows what it looks like. Some trim carries no identification markings and can only be identified visually. Some use a specific part number. A third way to identify trim is via an expert who knows your type of car.

Years ago, cars did not have as many shared parts. A restorer would have problems finding "1954 Pontiac" moldings unless he knew whether the car in need of them was a Chieftain or Star Chief. The Star Chief had a longer wheelbase and required longer body side moldings.

Paint puts an excellent finish on metal trim parts like the "catwalk" grilles on this '40 Ford. The advantages of painted auto trim include excellent corrosion resistance and a good appearance at low cost.

Holes in the sheet metal and bumper of this '41 Ford pickup suggest missing bright metal trim. The owner of this vehicle maintains an excellent research library that includes old Ford parts books that illustrate each trim piece.

The iconic white anodized "house siding" trim insert on the rear fender of the '57 Chevy Bel Air is an example of an "applied" finish. Fortunately for restorers of this popular, high-production car, reproductions are available.

Restoring the "hockey stick" side trim insert on this '57 Plymouth convertible won't be as easy as looking in a catalog for reproduction '57 Chevy parts. This piece has a distinctive texture with very thin horizontal ribs.

Restorer Jerry Kopecky, who specializes in six-figure, every-nut-and-bolt restorations of Chrysler fin cars, says it is cheap to have all of the original hardware—every nut and bolt from a car—cadmium-plated the way these were.

Visual Identification

To identify a trim piece, a drawing, photo, or sample is needed. A book, a sales brochure, or a factory photo may aid identification. If you spot a car like yours at a show, check with the owner to be sure it is stock.

Using Part Numbers

Parts catalogs show illustrations of trim parts and their part numbers. Aftermarket publishers put the same information in "crash books." Such sources provide a part number or Group Number that can help identify trim for your car. Stainless-steel trim moldings sometimes have numbers stenciled on the back. Some numbers are stamped on parts. The numbers often have "R" or "RH" if they fit the right-hand side of the car and "L" or "LH" if they fit the left-hand side. Reproduction parts' numbers rarely match the manufacturer's numbers.

A master parts catalog for your car is very good to have, whether you get an original or a reproduction. Such books are expensive but worth having. You may be able to get one on an online auction site like eBay for a reasonable price. In addition to listing part numbers, they illustrate the fasteners used for trim.

Parts Experts

Some people know what parts fit which cars. Many worked in the auto industry or repair business and dealt with parts. Others have been collecting cars and visiting junkyards for years.

Restorers tend to network at swap meets, car shows, cruise nights, and car clubs—and lately through Internet news groups. Vendors who sell old car parts should also know about the parts they sell.

Using the Intenet

The Internet has *not* proven a reliable method of finding needed parts unless they are in original factory boxes. Used parts and vintage aftermarket parts are often misidentified. Online sellers usually offer refunds if a part doesn't fit, but they will charge a restocking fee.

Many online sellers supply quality merchandise and identify their parts accurately, but others purchase inventory "closeouts" and wind up with lots of parts in unmarked boxes. Avoid listings that say "may fit" or "looks a lot like!" Other online sellers advertise cheap, fits-all-cars aftermarket accessories as factory options.

REPLACING MISSING TRIM

If your car is missing trim, you have three options: (1) fit new trim, (2) fit good used trim, or (3) recondition what you have. The availability of parts will vary from one car to another. With reproduction parts, you can almost build a complete Model A Ford, but you can't get as many reproduction parts for a Studebaker.

New Parts

There are three types of new parts. Never-used originals called NOS (new old stock) parts. These are desirable and expensive. NORS (new old replacement stock) parts are aftermarket parts made years ago. The quality varies and aftermarket trim parts are rare. A third category is the reproduction part. These are modern copies of old parts. The quality of reproduction parts can vary. NOS, NORS, and reproduction parts are found at swap meets, in ads in hobby magazines, in catalogs, and on the Internet.

Used Parts

Used original parts are gaining value. Techniques have been developed to recondition used parts. Worn parts that you kept years ago may now be worth money to companies that recondition them.

Some builders of hot rods and custom cars do a great job of using paint to cover parts originally plated. When going this route, it is important to use high-quality automotive-grade paints and to follow can instructions. *Eastwood*

The powder coating process used on Bolt Locker's powder coated small-block Chevy fuel-injection system and other engine parts uses static electricity to make the fine, dry powder of paint pigments cling to a part. Heat liquefies the powder, and as the part cools, the paint returns to a solid.

Bright trim was a status symbol. This blue '38 Packard Six has less trim than the red '38 Packard Eight shown on the next page. A close look will reveal different hood louver trim, smooth front and rear bumpers, and a lack of trim on top of the headlights.

This red '38 Packard Eight has more trim than the blue '38 Packard Six. A close look will reveal additional hood louver trim, grooved front and rear bumpers, and trim ornaments on top of the headlights.

Muscle car experts like Steve Bimbi of Nickey Chicago are familiar with the correct bright metal trim pieces for cars like this '70 Dodge Coronet R/T convertible. Asking the experts is faster than trying to find factory literature.

When to Restore Missing Trim

Restorers working on rare cars must rely on used parts. Nobody makes reproduction parts for a Hudson, and even some parts for MGs are not reproduced. Sometimes used parts are the restorer's only option. Reconditioning a used part to look new is cheaper than having a part custom manufactured. It is amazing how well some parts can be restored. Restorative processes have been developed to save parts that can't be found elsewhere. Some shops specialize in restoring subassemblies and have the parts and know-how to do a specific job.

BASIC CONCEPT OF THIS BOOK

You can work and polish much of the bright metal trim on your collector car right in your home garage, if you accumulate the proper supplies and tools and develop the necessary patience. You won't have to attend school, take special seminars, or work for 20 years as an expert's apprentice. But you do have to invest in some tools, buy all of the proper abrasives, arrange for a suitable place to work, and be ready to, as Matt Kokolis puts it, "sand until your arm feels like it's going to fall off."

There are nearly 60 rivets, 50 screws, and 40 nuts and fasteners used in the 1956–1967 Corvette hardtops that Matt restores at Glassworks: The Hardtop Shop. On top of that, there are dozens of bright metal moldings and trim pieces. As we watched Matt working in his shop near Pittsburgh, we were amazed to see him continue working on moldings that we would have thought we had ruined. Hammering the back side of the moldings initially leaves the front with a "pockmarked" or "textured" appearance, and we would have given up at that point. Matt, however, keeps going until all the dents are gone. He then sands the front of the piece with finer and finer sandpaper until it is totally smooth again. After buffing it with the proper rouge, it will look absolutely new. When he completes a vintage Corvette hardtop and reassembles it, the fiberglass "lid" shines like a jewel.

Matt Kokolis learned these skills as a teenager, back when he had very little personal interest in vintage 'Vettes. You can read the whole story at www.thehardtopshop.com. The important thing to realize is that means you can do this type of restoration yourself. All you really need is the focus and concentration that Matt brings to the job. If you can muster that up, you'll have no trouble learning how to restore auto trim.

The availability of NOS and reproduction parts will vary from car to car. If you needed trim for a '57 Lincoln Premiere two-door hardtop like this one, you might have to visit a salvage yard.

Reconditioning a used part to look new is cheaper than having a part custom manufactured. Restorative processes like stainless-steel buffing have been developed to save parts that can't be found.

TOOLS AND EQUIPMENT

"I'm always a little bit skeptical on giving folks information about stainless-steel restoration," Kokolis admitted. "I think you'll find that a lot of do-it-yourselfers don't have the tools that a professional stainless-steel restoration shop would have. There are two different directions to take here. Either you sand the hell out of the piece by hand and use a lightweight buffer to bring up the shine, or you have the proper equipment, like a sanding belt and high-speed buffer, to get pieces done in mass quantity."

Professional combo buffing kits are available for under $50 and high-speed buff motors cost as little as $160 from companies such as Eastwood. Buffing compounds for all types of metals, full-size and mini buffs, flap brushes, and polishes are other products you'll want to consider. Specialty plastic pry tools allow damage-free trim removal. Eastwood product specialist John Sloane says a good starting kit for home auto trim restoration could be put together for under $500.

Personal Safety and Protective Gear

The first time we used a buffing wheel to try to shine up a brass S.U. carburetor overflow tube, the buffing motor tore it out of our hands and flung it across the room. It flew so quickly that we didn't see where it landed and spent a half hour looking until we found it under a '48 Pontiac. If it had hit us—or the car—we would not be smiling about this incident!

Skip the goggles that make you sweat and leave most of your face unprotected. Get a full-face shield, throw in leather gloves, wear heavy work shoes, and buy a shop apron. As usual, avoid loose clothing and neck chains and like your mother said, tie your shoelaces. A hardhat isn't a bad idea, and earplugs are recommended.

ENDNOTES

1. *The Art of American Car Design: The Profession and Personalities,* C. Edson Armi, The Pennsylvania State University Press. 1988.

2. *Packard,* George H. Dammann and Jim Wren, (Crestline Imprint) Motorbooks International. 1996.

3. *The Art of American Car Design: The Profession and Personalities,* C. Edson Armi, The Pennsylvania State University Press. 1988.

Chapter 2
Types of Trim Damage

Restoring automotive trim and hardware involves reversing wear, environmental effects, and damage. The damage can occur in a number of ways, and both the type and degree of damage factor into the practicality of restoring the part.

Trim parts can have minor damage caused by normal vehicle use. This "wear and tear" includes tarnishing, light scratches, loose attachment, and dulling or discoloration. Given current hobby trends that favor the collecting of "survivor" vehicles, an owner may deem it wise—from a value standpoint—to leave wear and tear damage alone when it adds to a vehicle's "patina." On the other hand, there may be a point where excessive wear and tear detracts enough to make some buffing and polishing a wise choice.

The condition of the bright metal trim on vehicles like this '41 Ford convertible owned by Ron De Woskin can mean the difference between having a nice show car and having a consistent show winner.

Cars preserved with a few flaws or blemishes are popular now. George Bastounes' '38 Buick Century was part of the first Bloomington Gold Survivor event, even with its unrestored bright metal trim. *Jesse Gunnell*

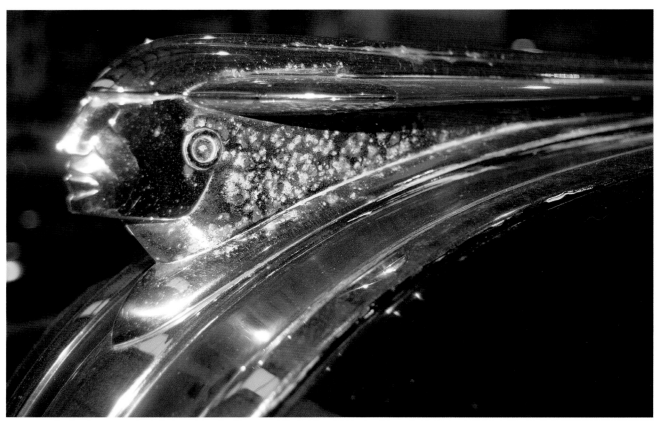

The elements can damage bright metal parts like this '48 Pontiac hood mascot. Moisture, excessive heat and cold, strong sunlight, wind, hail, and acid rain can all cause corrosion, even to cars stored inside.

Small dents, dings, and dimples, such as those on this molding, are what most restorers deal with when restoring trim. Here we see a crease type of dent on a 1948 Pontiac Streamliner belt molding.

Such decisions have to be made by the car owner. Even though a car with a couple of flaws may have the appeal of a "James Bond girl" with a limp or wart, there really is nothing quite as sharp looking as a collector vehicle with perfectly refinished trim that glitters brightly in the sunlight. Keep in mind that refreshing the looks of old trim does not reduce the originality of a vehicle if you do the job properly. In many cases, the restoration of trim parts—when no painting or replating is involved—is really just a matter of giving them a super good cleaning.

Even reversing the effects of light weathering or removing very minor surface damage (like a minor dent, ding, or dimple) is more like *maintenance* than heavy-duty restoration. These jobs can be done without destroying a vehicle's patina, as long as the finished piece does not look "too new" compared to the rest of the vehicle. If you can follow the art school rule of "working the whole canvas" to give the vehicle an overall even cosmetic appearance, you will wind up with a very nice car, truck, or motorcycle.

Of course, finding a vehicle that is not fully restored and has no trim damage is rare. Sunlight, acid rain, road debris,

parking lot bumps, doors opened in tight-fitting garages, kids' toys, bird droppings, tree sap, air pollution, exhaust smoke, and other everyday occurrences can chip away at a vehicle's newness.

There are five types of minor damage that typically show up on collector vehicles that are still very much worth restoring: (1) weathered trim parts, (2) trim parts with signs of minor impacts (dents, dings, and dimples), (3) trim parts twisted out of shape in collisions, (4) trim parts that were rusted or corroded, and (5) trim parts that were customized by previous owners.

WEATHERING OF METAL
The different effects of weather can cause serious damage to metal auto trim. Moisture, excessive heat and cold, strong sunlight, wind, hail, acid rain, and other environmental factors can promote corrosion or actually cause physical damage to the trim on a vehicle, sometimes even if it is stored inside.

There is a rule that everything brought from nature tries to go back to nature. Metal tries to go back to its natural state through an electrochemical degradation process known

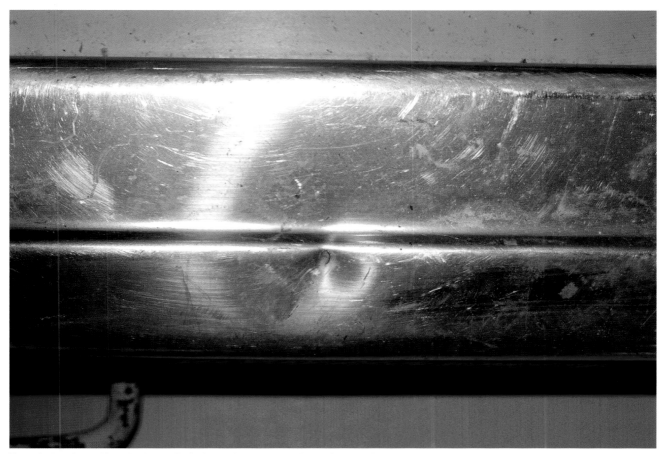

The original molding on this 1953–1954 Pontiac fender skirt has a dent, multiple scratches, and other wear and tear. When the car is restored, this molding will be replaced with an NOS piece, but it could also be restored.

All trim parts can undergo oxidation. The damage may vary from tarnished silver alloys to the pimpled pot metal in this '57 Buick taillight assembly. In salvage yards, you'll see rust in places you don't expect it.

as corrosion, in which the metal reacts with its environment. This process is accelerated by the presence of acids or bases (alkalis), and their presence can be encouraged by certain weather conditions.

Corrosion is actually caused by oxidation—the reaction of oxygen with the metal in the presence of moisture. Although it is most noticeable in iron and steel—metals that readily pit and flake because oxides do not adhere to them—corrosion occurs in all metals, even those considered "rust-resistant," which are used in making most auto trim. It's a fact that aluminum, a nonferrous metal—actually corrodes *faster* than iron, but the thin, continuous transparent layer of oxide formed on the surface of the aluminum then protects it from further corrosion. These layers can often be seen on aluminum car parts.

Copper is a more inactive metal and corrodes very slowly. This process produces a green-colored basic carbonate of copper. Similar corrosion appears on copper alloys like brass and bronze. Silver reacts with air, water, and hydrogen sulfide. Its degree of corrosion is very low and shows up in the form of black discoloration called tarnishing. Tarnishing is caused by the formation of silver sulfide.

A prior owner of this MG TF "customized" it by painting the hubcap center badges black (left). These were replaced with reproduction parts (right), but many times the only option is to restore the original parts.

Corrosion may attack bright plated trim parts if the surface is compromised by minute openings that allow air and moisture to get under the plating. The chrome on this MG TF taillight housing has been ruined.

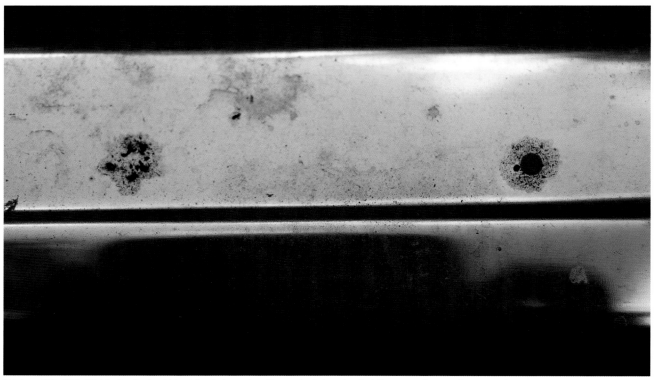

This is an NOS 1953–1954 Pontiac fender skirt molding that was stored in an unheated garden shed. You can see how small rust spots formed in places where air and moisture were able to reach the base metal.

In many cases, restoring a molding primarily involves cleaning it well. This is the same NOS 1953–1954 Pontiac fender skirt molding shown earlier after it was cleaned up and given a quick coat of wax.

Corrosion is like a cancer to metals. The initial oxidation of iron can be conducted through the metal, and the iron ions can diffuse through the water layer (water lying on top of the metal) to another point on the metal surface where oxygen is available. This is why corrosion can sometimes occur even far away from the spot where the iron starts pitting or eroding.

The presence of salt greatly speeds corrosion. This is known as sea weather corrosion. Seawater contains salt. The major ingredients of salt water are chlorides, sulphates, and sodium, which cause corrosion.

Weather conditions also affect corrosion. Rain can create a water layer that allows oxidation agents to diffuse. Collector cars that were once driven in snow probably accumulated road salt that promoted corrosion. Temperature also plays an important role in corrosion. For every 10-degree Celsius rise in the temperature of seawater, the corrosion rate doubles. Other weather-related factors that may play into the damage of metal auto trim are wind, hail, and air pollution.

DENTS, DINGS, AND DIMPLES

Minor surface damage, like small dents, dings, and dimples, are what most restorers will have to deal with. Typical dents include vertical creases across the surface of the molding, caused by opening the door into another object or having someone open their car door into the molding. If these things happen forcefully, the molding may flatten at the spot of impact, rather than simply crease.

Many trim moldings will be found to have flattened and "wrinkled" tips. This happens, for instance, when a front door molding is slightly out of place and its front tip catches on the trailing edge of the front fender when the door is opened. In addition to damaging the molding tip, this may chip the paint on the edge of the door.

Such accidents tend to affect the attachment of the molding, since there may be clips under the flattened area. Even door alignment may be affected or the edge of the fender may be bent. It may be hard to believe that the car's DPO

Alloys of silver, as used in this MG TF rearview mirror, react with air, water, and hydrogen sulfide. When they corrode, it shows up as tarnishing, a black discoloration caused by the formation of silver sulfide.

The owners of these Austin-Healey 3000s are wise to protect the cars' interiors from rain during a show. Weather conditions can aid the deterioration of metal auto trim on the outside and inside of an old car.

(dreaded previous owner) didn't take care of minor problems right away, but some people live with trim snags for years.

Dings and dimples in trim moldings are usually shallow, pinpoint indentations that can be caused by such things as flying road debris, stones, or fallen tools or garage items like rakes or shop brooms. Sometimes a body shop or glass shop repairing another part will accidentally cause a ding. A person leaning against the car while wearing a belt buckle can create a dimple in the metal.

Most old cars do have a couple of dinged or dimpled moldings, and the cause is usually stones on the road being thrown up against the car. This will typically occur to a rocker panel molding or a fender skirt molding on the lower part of the car.

Minor dents, dings, and dimples are among the easiest and cheapest imperfections to repair, and dealing with them can greatly enhance a vehicle's appearance.

COLLISION DAMAGE

Collision damage is the result of impact caused by a vehicle hitting or being hit by an object. The object is often another vehicle. The metal is damaged because it is subjected to a stronger force than it has the ability to resist. Unlike normal wear, collision damage results from an accident and is usually unpredictable. Since no two accidents are exactly the same, the processes used to repair damage will vary.

The force of an accident changes the trim's shape. It also changes the shape of surrounding metal. There are five ways to change the shape of metal. It can be (1) displaced, (2) bent, (3) buckled, (4) upset, or (5) stretched. Different repair procedures are used for each type of damage. On large panels, it's easy to spot the damage, but on trim pieces, similar damage occurs on smaller surfaces.

Displaced metal is not bent or distorted by impact. Instead, it is pushed out of position when other areas are buckled. If the strain that causes the buckling can be taken care of, the displaced metal pops back into position. You may see displacement when cars with large trim panels—like gravel shields or '57 Chevy rear fender inserts—are involved in a crash.

Bent parts result from "fender benders." Collision causes irregular folds in metal. When metal folds, its outer surface

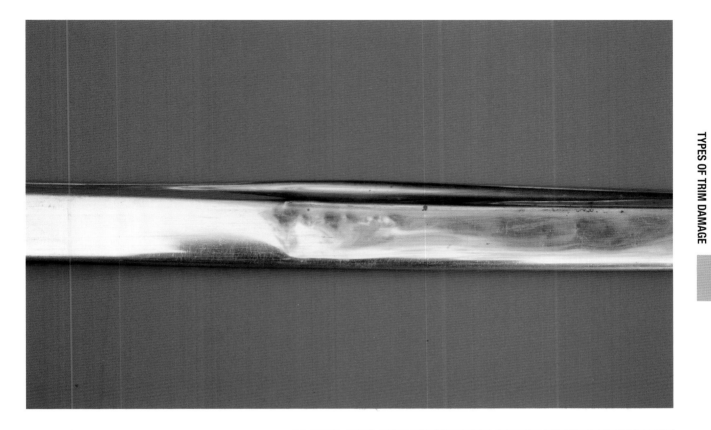

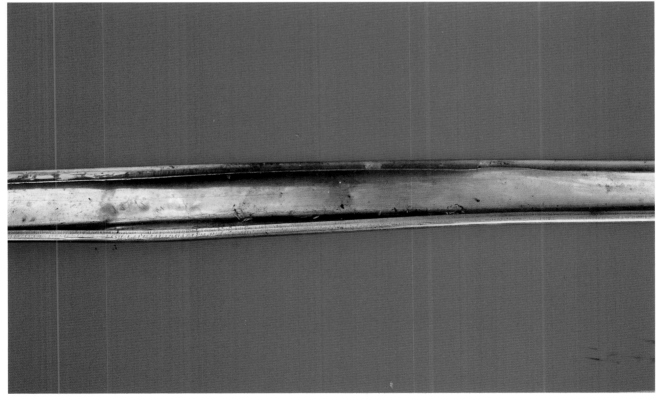

The removal of dents, dimples, and dings caused by door slamming and stone throwing enhances the looks of classic cars. As you can see, such damage affects the front (top) and rear (bottom) of a trim molding.

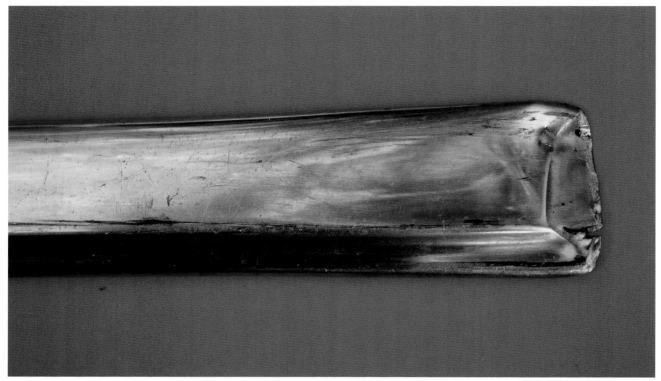

Trim moldings may have flattened or "wrinkled" tips. This can be caused by a front door molding being slightly out of place so that its front tip catches on the trailing edge of the front fender when the door opens.

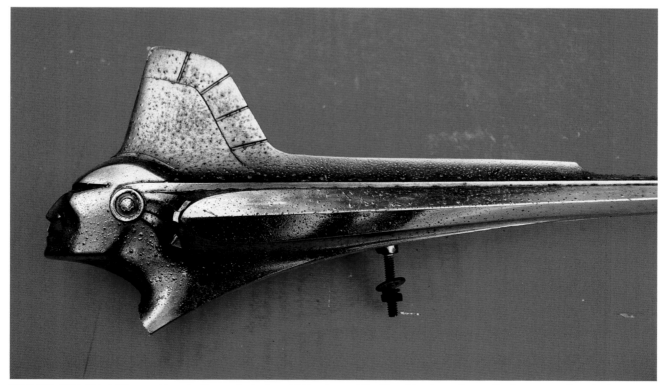

The chrome-plated pot metal this mascot is made of is prone to pimples and flaking chrome plating. These things happen because the cheap, porous alloy under the plating is unstable and oxidizes easily.

stretches and its inner surface shrinks. The metal changes shape. Bending is fixed by applying a force to the metal that reverses the bending. The closer you can get to applying an exactly equal and opposite force to the point of impact, the better the repair will be.

Buckles in metal trim parts are caused by the metal undergoing a "rolling" action after an impact occurs. A curved ridge is created at the point of impact and moves outward to a point at which the metal resists additional curving. This resistance to further bending causes a strain and the metal buckles. If the cause of the strain can be removed, the metal can be "unbuckled." Buckled metal is under tension— and when you remove the tension, you can straighten it.

An upset takes place when opposing forces push against a small area of metal, causing the surface area to shrink, while the thickness of the area actually increases. An upset can cause an "oil canning" effect, where metal pops in and out like a tin oil can, although other things like stretching can cause this. The use of proper repair procedures can keep upsets from occurring.

Stretching takes place when a metal's shape is changed by applying enough force to elongate a portion of it and make it thinner. This increases the metal's surface area. A gouged piece of trim has been stretched. This type of damage can be repaired by shrinking or by applying body filler. On bright metal trim, shrinking is best.

RUST AND CORROSION

Earlier we talked about the weathering of auto trim and the process involved when metal oxidizes or corrodes. We learned that even so-called "no-rust" metals corrode, creating a transparent layer of oxide on the surface of the metal that protects it from further corrosion.

Thanks to this coating, you're unlikely to find rusty aluminum or stainless-steel parts. However, there are still a number of ways rust and corrosion can cause problems to the trim on your vehicle. Think of some of the older vehicles you have seen at salvage yards. It's likely you've noticed some that have trim parts with pimpled or flaking off chrome plating,

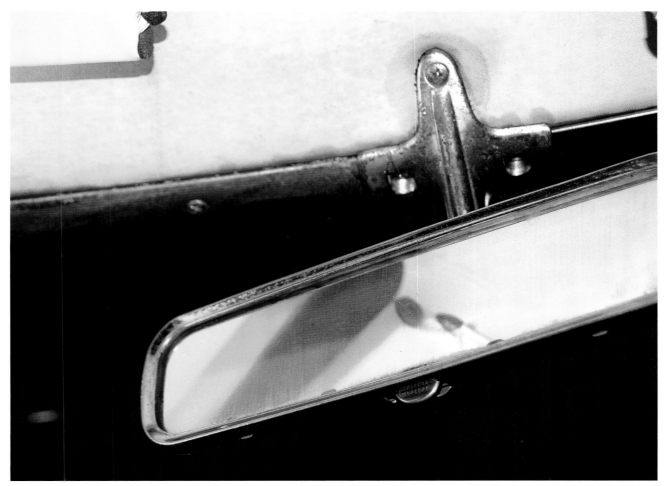

There is probably lots of copper in the base metal used to make these '53 Pontiac inner windshield moldings. The chalky green coating that forms when the car is kept in storage is probably carbonate of copper.

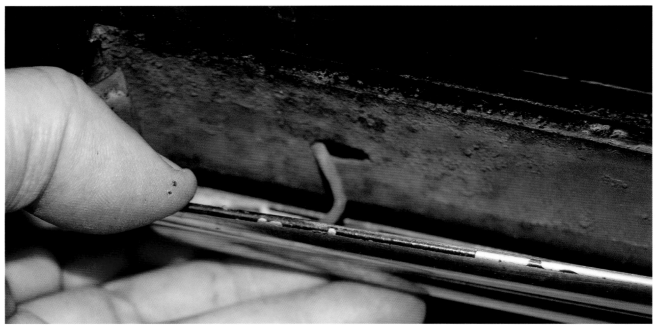

As you can see, the clips holding this '48 Pontiac rocker molding in place are not made of no-rust metal. They have been attacked by corrosion and, as a result, the moldings are loose fitting and rattly.

1947-58 GRILLE PARTS (Passenger)

YEAR	Assy. 1.266	Rnfct. Assy. 1.266	Deflector 1.266	HORIZONTAL MOULDING Upper 1.268	Center 1.268	Lower 1.268	Moulding Side 1.268	VERTICAL MOULDING Center 1.268	Inter. 1.268	Outer 1.268	Park. Lamp Panel 1.266
1947	3847456-R 3690280-Ctr. 3847455-L			3687410							
1948	3847456-R 3690280-Ctr. 3847455-L	.		3687410				3687150			
1949		3688406		3688269	3688271	3693966		3688381	3688382	3688384-R 3688383-L	
1950		3692600 3694926*		3688269	3688271	3693966			3692604-R 3692603-L	3688384-R 3688383-L	
1951		3694926*	3694928-Ctr. 3694933-Lwr.	3699630	3694927	3694930	3699644-R 3699643-L				
1952		3694926*	3699636-Ctr. 3694933-Lwr.	3699630	3699632	3694930	3699644-R 3699643-L	3699633	3699638-R 3699637-L	3699652-R 3699651-L	
1953		3701630*	3697859-Ctr. 3697860-Lwr.	3703145	3703146	3703147	3703150-R 3703149-L	3703148		3703152-R 3703151-L	
1954		3701630*		3705305	3705306		3705308-R 3705307-L	3705313	3705312-R 3705311-L	3705310-R 3705309-L	
1955	3709690	3710500		3711156		3711158	3711162-R 3711161-L				
1956	3721025	3721537		3721984		3720864	3721988-R 3721987-L				3731830-R 3731829-L
1957	3737253 3738775†			3730805	3729340⊕		3730804-R 3730803-L				
1958	3747202			3744732			3742608-R 3742607-L				

*Header Bar Reinforcement.   †Gold finish Bel Air.   ⊕Includes Park. Lamp Panel.

This chart from a Chevrolet master parts catalog can be referred to for factory part numbers for grille components for 1947–1958 models. It can be used to authenticate that a restorer uses the correct trim pieces.

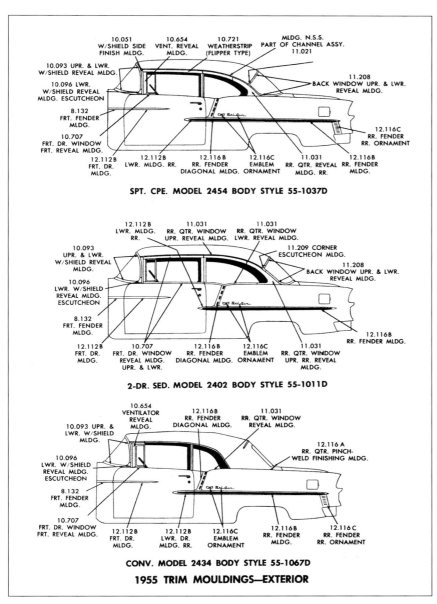

1955 TRIM MOULDINGS—EXTERIOR

Master parts catalog illustrations show the correct trim and moldings for a '55 Bel Air two-door sedan, '55 Bel Air hardtop, and '55 convertible. The catalog will help you determine the trim pieces used on your car.

with an ugly and chalky-looking green coating, with rusty clips and fasteners, or even with a layer of surface rust.

Not all trim parts are made of no-rust metals. Some are made of pot metal, which the automakers plated to create hood mascots, headlight "doors," fender top moldings, logo badges, and model name scripts. Pot metal (AKA die cast or monkey metal) is an alloy of cheap, low-melting point metals used to make inexpensive castings quickly. Automakers used pot metal because it was a fast, easy way to make parts. No sophisticated foundry equipment or specialized molds were needed. However, the unstable pot metal parts broke easily and were prone to oxidizing under their chrome plating, causing pimples to form or causing the plating to flake off in large pieces.

Other trim pieces seem to corrode in unexpected ways. We own a 1953 Pontiac hardtop that has bright metal surrounds on the inside of the windshield. Although these appear to be stainless steel, there is corrosion on the pieces and a chalky green coating forms if they are not polished. While we have not subjected the trim to scientific analysis, there is probably a lot of copper in the alloy, and the green coating is carbonate of copper.

Tarnishing was mentioned earlier. This is the black discoloration that occurs when silver sulfide forms on silver-based metals. In salvage yards, you will see vintage vehicles with trim pieces so badly tarnished they seem impossible to restore.

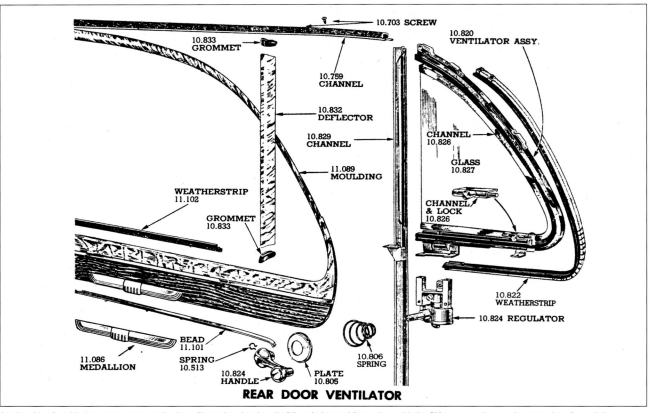

REAR DOOR VENTILATOR

10.703 SCREW
10.833 GROMMET
10.820 VENTILATOR ASSY.
10.759 CHANNEL
10.832 DEFLECTOR
10.829 CHANNEL
CHANNEL 10.826
GLASS 10.827
11.089 MOULDING
WEATHERSTRIP 11.102
GROMMET 10.833
CHANNEL & LOCK 10.826
10.822 WEATHERSTRIP
10.824 REGULATOR
11.086 MEDALLION
BEAD 11.101
SPRING 10.513
10.824 HANDLE
PLATE 10.805
10.806 SPRING

Another thing found in the master parts catalog is an illustration showing all of the window moldings, along with the GM group numbers and part numbers for such items.

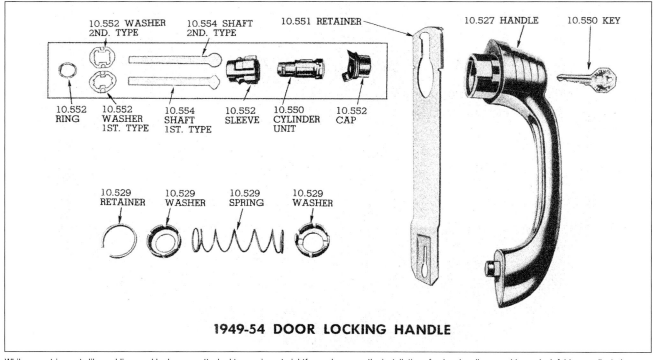

1949-54 DOOR LOCKING HANDLE

10.552 WASHER 2ND. TYPE
10.554 SHAFT 2ND. TYPE
10.551 RETAINER
10.527 HANDLE
10.550 KEY
10.552 RING
10.552 WASHER 1ST. TYPE
10.554 SHAFT 1ST. TYPE
10.552 SLEEVE
10.550 CYLINDER UNIT
10.552 CAP
10.529 RETAINER
10.529 WASHER
10.529 SPRING
10.529 WASHER

While many trim parts like moldings and badges are attached to cars in a straightforward manner, the installation of a door handle assembly can look fairly complicated, as illustrated in the master parts catalog.

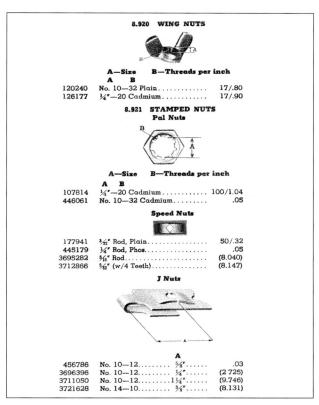

Until automakers started using tape or adhesives, most trim parts were held on vintage vehicles with special clips or fasteners. Hood mascots, badges, scripts, trunk ornaments, hood ornaments, and nameplates were usually attached with studs or screws. Although the trim itself may be rust resistant, these fasteners rarely were. As the fasteners corrode, they can cause problems.

Finally, during salvage yard excursions, you have probably seen trim parts that are covered in surface rust. If the underlying part has a high enough iron content, it may rust once the shiny surface plating deteriorates.

CUSTOMIZING

The customization of trim parts by a collector vehicle's DPO (dreaded previous owner) can be a big problem for the restorer. If certain trim is removed or replaced with a piece from another vehicle or an aftermarket piece, the only thing that can be done is to replace it with an original, whether it is NOS or used. Although such a replacement may be considered part of the restoration of the overall vehicle, it doesn't involve any restoration work to the piece itself.

In other cases, previous owners may paint a plated piece, drill additional holes in a piece, or even change the shape of a piece with filler or a tool. In these cases, it may be easier to restore the old trim than to replace a rare piece.

The extent of the changes made will also affect whether the trim can be restored. For example, if a molding was

Selecting the proper fasteners and clips for attaching bright metal trim to a car gets easier if you have a master parts catalog. Such items are listed in the "standard parts" section of the old parts book.

There will be some detail differences in trim applications between a 1959 Dodge Coronet Lancer, a fancier 1959 Dodge Coronet Royal Lancer, and a top of the line 1959 Dodge Coronet Custom Royal Lancer.

shortened with a plasma cutter or ground down with a rotary tool, it may be virtually impossible to restore it to its original condition. However, it should be possible to fill a hole drilled in the piece or even to remove old body filler. Of course, if the piece is easily replaceable, why bother restoring it at all? You might be able to find one at a swap meet or in a catalog.

If you're not sure if the trim on your car was customized or otherwise changed, you'll need to find reference materials that tell you or show you what trim was proper for your year, make, and model. Factory parts catalogs and master parts catalogs should include sections with charts describing the trim for each model produced in certain years. You may find part numbers or illustrations of some trim parts.

Be sure you know the exact model of your car. There will be some detail differences in trim between a 1959 Dodge Coronet Lancer, a 1959 Dodge Coronet Royal Lancer, and a 1959 Dodge Coronet Custom Royal Lancer. To make matters worse, customizers sometimes switch trim between such models that are based on the same basic car. The parts books will tell you the correct trim application. Shop manuals, sales literature, factory photos, and automotive history books can also be a big help. As you use such sources to learn about your collector vehicle, you may find that certain trim was optional for your model.

You may find that certain trim—such as this illuminated Pontiac hood mascot—was optional for your car. Keep in mind that each additional dress-up item will add to the cost of your restoration.

When cars are left outside to endure lots of hard use and abuse, the trim parts—even those made of so-called no-rust metals like stainless steel—can wind up looking pretty rough.

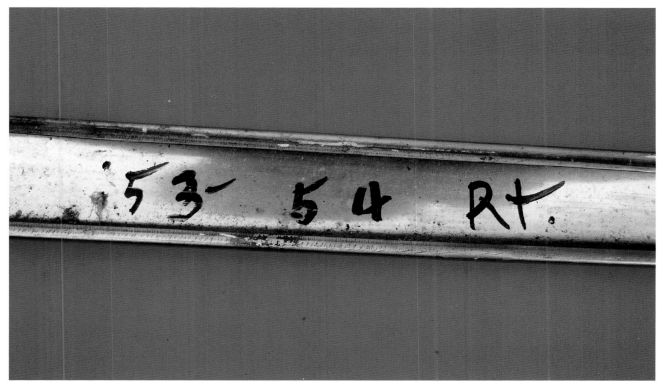

The backsides of many trim moldings may not be given the same rust-resistant finishes as the front sides. By the way, take identification info written on old moldings using marker pens with a grain of salt.

Chapter 3
Introduction to the Restoration of Metal Moldings

Matt Kokolis of Glassworks, in Crescent, Pennsylvania, is an artist at buffing metal. When Matt was a kid, his dad insisted that he restore the trim on early Corvette hardtops when he'd rather have been hanging out with friends. Now Matt does it for a living. When he sands, buffs, and polishes metal, he slips off into his own world. Even though Matt is all serious concentration when working, he has a simple view of the job.

"I think that, generally, most folks I speak to are at home trying to do this," he says. "They just need to spot a dent,

pick it out with a lightweight hammer, file it flat, and then go through various grits of sandpaper—80-grit for heavy-duty pieces and, normally, 150 for all other trim pieces (just to help get the spot level). They then use 220-, 400-, 600-, and 1,500-grit to work out all of the scratches with wet sanding. Once their arms feel like they're going to fall off, they'll know they're done. Then, they can pick up a small cotton buff wheel and either green or white rouge. After attaching the buff wheel to a grinder, they'll be able to buff out the light remaining scratches."

Matt Kokolis of Glassworks is an artist when it comes to restoring trim. When working metal, he drifts off into his own world. His focused approach to the job at hand seems to be one of his "trade secrets."

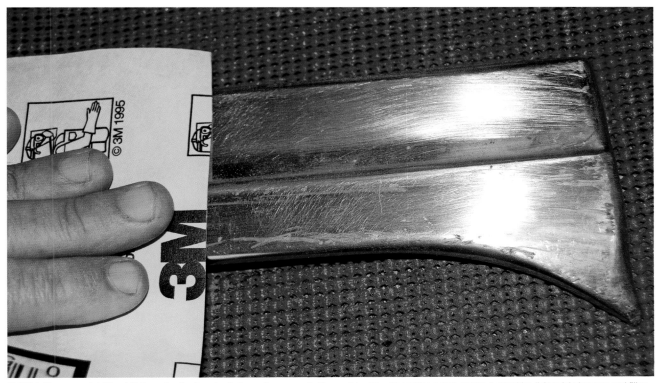

Matt Kokolis sums up bright metal trim restoration in a simple three-step approach. He says it begins with spotting a dent, picking it out with a lightweight hammer, and filing the repaired area flat. Next comes sanding, with 150-grit the starting point for most trim. Go to 220-, 400-, 600-, and 1,500-grit to remove scratches with wet sanding. Matt says "stick with it until your arm feels like it's going to fall off."

The last step is using a high-speed buffing motor—like this one with a very effective metal safety guard in use at Custom Plating Specialties. Such motors can be fitted with a variety of buffing pads, each designed for different compounds and metals. *Eastwood*

The cars in front of the cans illustrate some of the many colors that these automotive finishes come in. Epoxy primers and base coat clear coat systems are popular today. Some modern finishes may require use of a catalyst or an activator. *Eastwood*

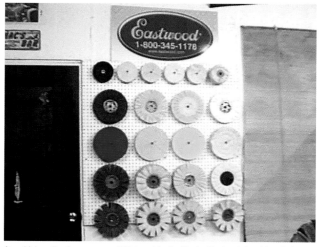

As vehicle collecting grew, so did interest in the "lost art" of metalworking. Today, suppliers like Eastwood sell metalworking tools and supplies. This display illustrates a wide variety of buffs and flap wheels. *Eastwood*

TWO GENERAL WAYS TO RESTORE METAL AUTO TRIM

Sanding and buffing stainless-steel moldings and trim, as described above by Matt Kokolis, is the main restoration technique that this book will focus on, but there are other traditional skills to learn. In addition, new technologies are coming down the pike that may be of interest to certain car builders. For example, at the recent Bloomington Gold Corvette swap meet, M+M Custom Finishes of Bristol, Illinois, was promoting a method of putting custom woodgrain and carbon weave finishes on metal trim parts with a water transfer printing system. This would be of particular interest to builders of "Resto-Mod" Corvettes (cars with restored original bodies and modern, high-tech running gear).

Sanding and buffing a Corvette top molding constitutes metalworking and refinishing. When M+M decorates metal with its water pressure application process, it uses a top coating that provides a new, yet changed, appearance. Each of these approaches can involve a number of skills or processes. Repairing can usually be done in the home restoration shop. Top coating and plating usually require special equipment and must be "farmed out," but it's good to know what's involved.

Metalworking and Refinishing

When working metal and refinishing it, restorers rely on skills that were nearly lost arts not long ago. In our "throwaway society" there was not much interest in restoration. Only people in specialized trades, like jewelry makers, restored bright metal items. Then, as the old-car hobby grew, interest in metalworking returned. Today, companies like Eastwood sell metalworking tools and supplies.

Sanding, buffing, and polishing are the primary skills involved in auto trim restoration, but some jobs may require metal or plastic body filler to restore a rare ornament or badge. If a hard to replace body molding is dented, fillers may be required to repair the damage. Working with each type of filler requires a different skill set. Plastic and fiberglass fillers are better than ever, but using metal filler is "old skool" cool.

In some cases, trim parts may need to be fabricated in sheet metal or by casting them. Trim parts will have to be drilled to restore attaching screws or studs. The use of a hammer and dolly is another metalworking method that you may need to learn. Parts hurt in a collision may need to be bent back into shape without damaging them. See Chapter 5.

Top Coating or Plating

Top coating means putting something on top of metal trim to restore its looks. Paint, powder coating, wood veneering, and pressure transfers are some examples of popular top coatings. When the covering is a thin oxide layer over polished metal, the part is plated. Usually, the plating material is chromium. You can get commercial-grade plating or show-grade and there is a difference in cost. Plating plastic trim parts, which is done with a vacuum plating process, is a special skill.

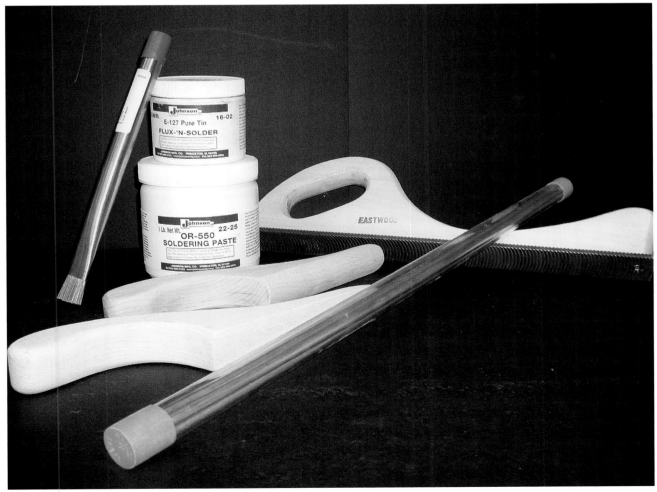

Today's plastic fillers work very well, but hobbyists consider lead body filler to be "old skool cool." Eastwood sells six body solder kits including paddles, files, tallow, tinning butter, plus an instructional DVD.

Some top coating, such as painting, is done at home. Companies like Eastwood, Northern Tool, and Harbor Freight, sell home powder coating systems for hobbyists willing to invest in such equipment. A hobbyist can also learn wood veneering techniques.

While in theory metal plating could be done on a small scale by a hobbyist who paid attention in high school chemistry class, this is really one of those "don't try this at home" things. In a practical sense, this is a job you will want to farm out to a professional plating shop. Such businesses have specialized equipment and skills, not to mention systems needed to meet environmental regulations.

THREE TYPES OF METAL

The way in which you rework and refinish metal has a great deal to do with the type of metal you're dealing with and how skilled you become in shaping metal. After years of working as a teacher, Steve Hamilton of Hamilton Classics, in Fond du Lac, Wisconsin, (S57Chevy@charter.net) started restoring cars and grew interested in metalworking and sheet, metal fabrication.

"I already had some knowledge of metal working skills," Hamilton recalls. "But my real proficiency in that area developed after 2001." He credits two organizations, MetalShapers (www.MetalShapers.org) and MetalMeet (www.MetalMeet.com), with teaching him how to become a master craftsman in this field. Hamilton pointed out that such organizations even hold weeklong meets where informative workshops on metalworking are conducted.

The correct way to restore metal auto trim depends on the properties of the metals you're working with. A soft metal, such as aluminum, can be easy to shape. A hard metal, like stainless steel, can be difficult to bend or form. Trim parts made of both soft and hard metal can be obtained with a variety of bright finishes from a satinlike surface to a highly polished surface. There may not be much scientific difference between bright metal and dull metal, but in trimming a car, the *applications* for each differ.

This photo of an expert repairing a body side molding by working it with a light Repouse hammer and small trim anvil illustrates one of the important properties of metal—its ability to be easily reshaped. *Eastwood*

Brass—a member of the "soft metals" family—was commonly used to make bright trim pieces for early automobiles like this beautiful Buick Model 10 at the 2008 Atlantic City Classic Car Auction.

Use lighter tools on softer metals. Eastwood's Repouse hammer weighs 8 ounces. The tiny trim anvil has conical and pyramid horns and a square flat center 5¼ inches long by 1 in. wide by 2⅞ inches tall. *Eastwood*

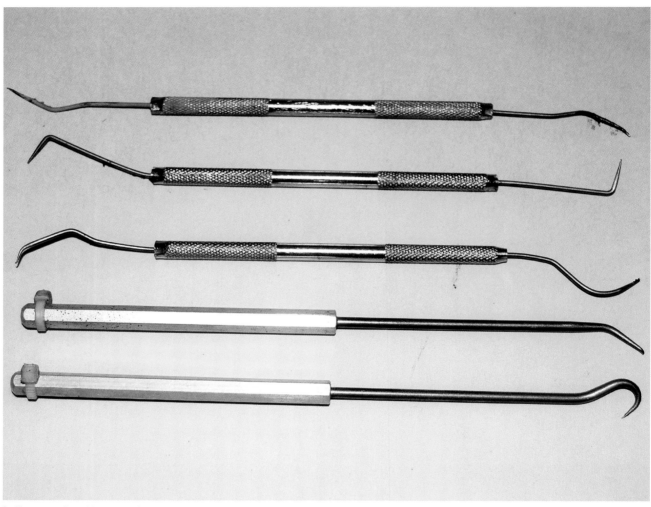

Stuffing your toolbox with a variety of dental picks is a good idea, and they can come in very handy. You may need to get into small nooks and crannies when you're restoring bright metal auto trim.

After the piece has been filed and sanded with various grits of sandpaper, you will need to polish it with buffing wheels on a single- or multispeed buff motor, using the proper rouges, to get it as smooth as you can. *Eastwood*

Soft Metal

Soft metals include aluminum, copper, brass, lead, gold, and silver. Of these, aluminum is the one that you'll encounter most often in auto trim applications. However, brass trim is commonly found on cars built up to about 1916, and all of the other soft metals (including the precious ones like gold and silver) have been used to dress up some cars.

Aluminum is restored using the same techniques used to do stainless steel, but working aluminum will take less time, and you must be careful to avoid sanding or buffing aluminum too thin. To avoid damaging the metal, use finer sandpaper or gentler buffing rouges made especially for aluminum. Straightening aluminum and other soft metals requires less force and very careful use of hammers and prying tools. The lighter the metal, the lighter in weight and smaller in size the metalworking tools should be. Such metals should also be protected when you clamp them down. Use cardboard or foam on the jaws of your vise.

Aluminum and other soft metals can readily tear when a car trimmed with them is involved in a crash. Tears can be repaired by first working the trim piece back to a near original shape with punches and chisels, then welding the damaged area using special aluminum welding wire and welding gas.

Hard Metal

The "hard" metals that you'll find yourself dealing with most in auto trim applications are stainless steel and die cast. The restoration process starts with removing the trim, cleaning the piece, and inspecting it after it is clean. You will use a marking pen to mark the flaws you need to repair such as dents, creases, bends, scratches, and tarnished or otherwise discolored areas.

As for tools, you'll be using hammers, dollies, anvils, punches, chisels, files, various types of pliers, dental picks, vises, and even presses on occasion, to straighten and repair the trim. You should have a measuring device and a straight edge handy. Inside and outside calipers can help you measure the width of a molding for straightness.

You are going to be using these tools to pick out dents and repair other damage to the piece. You will also be returning it to its original factory shape by removing bends, curvatures, twists, and waviness. Keep in mind that a half-finished piece being hammered back into shape might have an appearance that's discouraging to an amateur. It isn't really until the sanding, polishing, and refinishing is completed that the trim piece looks like new again.

Bright Metal

Bright metal isn't really a type of metal. Instead, you might say that it's a state of metal. Both soft metals and hard metals can be polished to look bright and lustrous, although the techniques used to polish different metals will be different.

The wheels, spokes, and bright metal fender on this Norton Atlas 750 motorcycle illustrate how well metals can shine with proper care and polishing.

A bright, shiny appearance results when rays of light refract (bounce back) off a surface at the same angle. If the surface is rough, it actually has hills and valleys on it and the light rays will bounce in every which way. The smoother the surface is, the more the rays will refract at the same angle. To make metal auto trim look new again, you need to get its surface "baby butt" smooth.

This smoothness is achieved by using abrasives to literally *grind* the surface smoother and smoother. To do this, you start with coarse abrasives and then progress through finer and finer grits. A variety of abrasives are used, from sandpapers to different types of rouge to very fine polishes.

After the surface is made as smooth and polished as possible, you will want to protect the bright finish you have achieved on the metal. This can be done with wax or clear top coats. Different techniques are used for different metals. No-rust metals like stainless steel need less protection than aluminum, which oxidizes quickly, but surface protection is always a good idea.

IMPORTANT PROPERTIES OF METAL

The restorer should know something about the general properties of metal if he or she plans to work with them. Metals are strong, dense, and hard materials and, except for mercury, exist as solids at room temperature. They can be polished to a shiny finish. Metals do a good job of conducting heat and electricity and these characteristics are related to their high melting points. As exhibited by bells, you can make sounds by striking metal (sometimes very nice sounds). You can also work metal to change its shape.

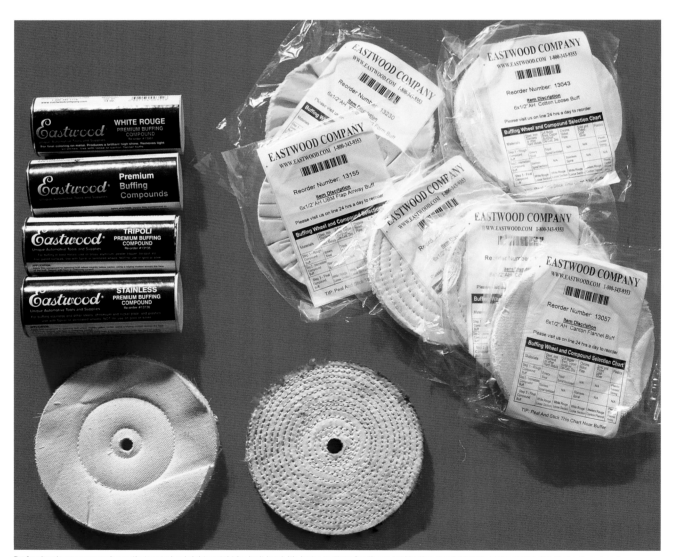

Professionals say over and over that restoring bright metal trim isn't hard. It's just a matter of patience and having the right tools and supplies, like these rouges and buff wheels.

When the job of restoring bright metal trim is done properly, you'll find yourself with a pile of used-up sandpaper and a sore arm from hours and hours of sanding by hand.

When hammering out dents results in a piece of trim that looks like this, you and I might give up hope and quit. Matt Kokolis, who did the hammering in this case, knows better.

Mike Freund of Classics Plus, Ltd., a North Fond du Lac, Wisconsin, shop, keeps a supply of rouges and an extra buff wheel nearby as he works on buffing a couple of pieces. *Jesse Gunnell*

The properties of different metals guide their application in different ways. Lead melts easily and can be readily used to make castings. Stainless steel resists rust and is perfect for automotive trim use. Aluminum's light weight makes it attractive for automotive use—especially today. But since it is shiny and easy to shape, it is also suitable for making automotive trim parts.

Metallurgists create alloys with unique properties. Aluminum, chromium, copper, iron, magnesium, nickel, titanium, and zinc are commonly used in making alloys. Stainless and galvanized steel are handy rust-resistant alloys. Aluminium alloys are great for purposes that demand both strength and light weight. Copper-nickel alloys resist corrosion. Many alloys now in use were not available when classic cars were new, but will be important to future hobbyists.

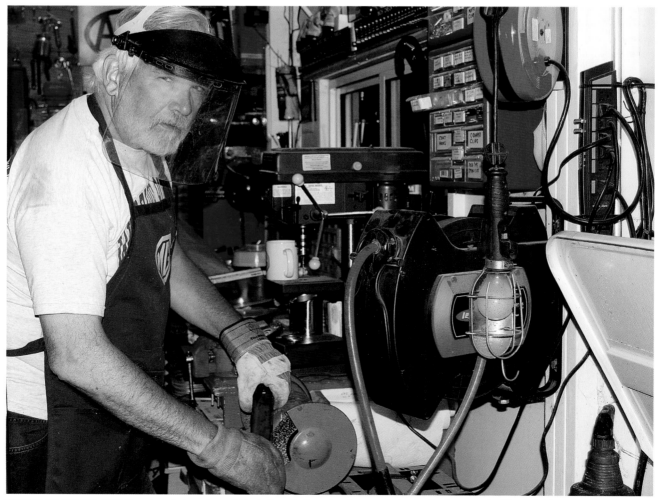

For safety, get a full-face shield, throw in work gloves (nonmatching in the author's case), and wear work shoes and a shop apron. Avoid loose clothing and jewelry. A hard hat and earplugs are also recommended. *Jesse Gunnell*

Chapter 4
Proper Removal and Replacement of Trim Moldings

As we've seen so far, the system for restoring bright metal trim is quite simple: You hammer out dents, file the metal flat, sand it smooth, and buff it to make the metal lustrous again. We are going to keep going over and over this process throughout this book, using different chapters to show how to do each step like an expert.

We can't do the steps with the trim still on the car. Dents are hammered out from the *back side* of the trim. You could possibly sand portions of a molding while it is on the car, but it's not the way to do it right and you risk sanding off body paint. Likewise, you could do some on-the-car buffing with a small buff on a rotary tool, but it would be impossible to work the edges to give the piece uniform luster.

To do a professional job of restoring trim, we have to remove it. There are several dangers in this, like the problem of damaging trim, especially if it's made of a soft metal like aluminum. Another big danger is breaking the hardware or pins that attach the trim to the car. Clips and bolts can grow weak from rust, while studs extending from the back of trim items such as name badges, are easy to break off. You can glue the badge on, but the best approach is to keep the studs intact.

Cars have been made for over 100 years. During that time, a large variety of clips and attaching hardware has been designed to hold trim on vehicles. Five designs are shown here.

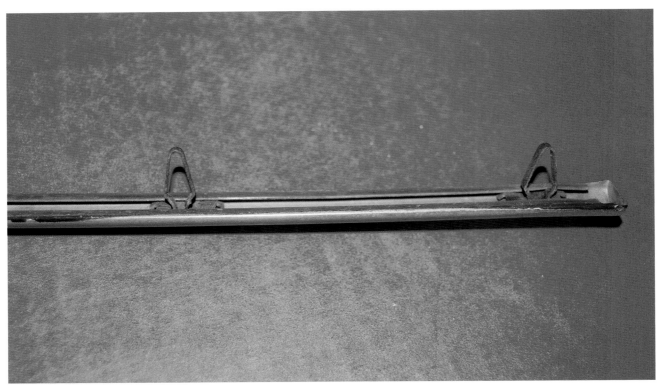

V-shaped clips held this molding on a '57 MG Magnette. The bases of the clips slide into slots on the back of the molding. The "V" gives a little bit, so it can be pushed into body holes before it springs back.

This clip has two prongs that push into holes in the car's body. The bent "spring arm" is designed to slide into the retaining lip on the back side of the molding at the spot where the lip widens.

To remove body molding and other trim without damaging it or breaking the fasteners that hold it on requires knowledge and tools. If we know the properties of the metal in the piece we're removing, we have a good idea of how much prying it can take. If the trim is made of soft metal, we'll know it scratches easily, and we can take extra precautions to avoid hurting it. Along the same lines, if we get familiar with the design of the common clips and fasteners, we'll know how to take more of them off without breaking them.

As with any type of work on a car, it's important to have the right tools and products to do the job. The basic tools and rust busters used in removing trim are pretty common, but we can also invest in some inexpensive specialty items, like plastic pry tools, if we want to do a better job.

TRIM ATTACHMENT METHODS

Today, most auto body moldings and trim are plastic pieces attached to cars with glue, with adhesive tape, or with plastic pegs that snap into holes in the body. In the "good old days" when trim was made of bright metal, automakers used clips and screws to hold trim on a car.

The job of attaching the trim had two aspects to it. First, there had to be a way to hold the fastener to the trim piece. For instance, a molding might be designed with bent over edges so, a clip could be snapped under the lip on the back side. Other trim pieces, like badges, might have studs cast into them or blind holes tapped into them to accept pins with a machine screw thread.

Once the fastener was affixed to the trim, the second aspect was attaching the trim-and-fastener assembly to the car. To accomplish this, the clip that fit into the lip on the back of the molding had to have a screw that passed through holes in the body and fastened on the back side. In the case of a badge, the studs or machine screws had to pass through holes in the body and accept a nut or Tinnerman nut on the inner side of the panel.

A small flat-blade screwdriver is used to push the clip into the retaining lip on the back of the molding. Old molding clips get rusty, but they may still be useable, and this can save you money.

There have been hundreds of different types of clips and fasteners made to hold trim on cars. The ones that you see most are snap-in-place clips, bolt-on clips, and "spring V" clips. However, you will find that fasteners used in the 1920s vary in design from those on 1960s cars. And though you are probably familiar with the clips that American automakers used, if you work on a British sports car, a German luxury sedan, or a Czechoslovakian Tatra, you're likely to run into fastener designs that you never encountered before.

A number of suppliers sell clips, fasteners, and molding bolts at swap meets and probably carry the majority of hardware you'll need to attach trim to any car from the muscle car era up. If you need to replace older fasteners or specialty items not seen every day, get in touch with Restoration Specialties & Supply, Inc. (www.restorationspecialties.com), of Windber, Pennsylvania, or Mr. G's Enterprises of Fort Worth, Texas (www.mrgusa.com). These vendors can help you identify exactly what you need and supply it in most cases.

TRIM REMOVAL METHODS AND TOOLS

When removing auto trim, begin by looking at the back side of the panel to see what fasteners were used. Sometimes the fasteners will be hidden behind other panels. You may need to remove parts to reach them. Fasteners can be snapped, bolted, or riveted to the car or held on by a thin prong under tension. Near the edge of a panel, you may find screws holding a clip that slides into a molding to fasten it in place. Look for these in door striker plates and hinges.

Removing a bolted-on molding may require removing small nuts and washers on the back side of a panel. You may find that the bolt that passes through the car body is part of a clip with a prong, spring, or wire that puts tension on it to hold it under a lip on the back of the molding. Use a tool like a small screwdriver, small needle-nose pliers, or a dental pick to relieve the tension so that the clip can be twisted and removed.

This fastener is used at the end of '57 MG Magnette moldings for secure attachment. It has a small nut, bolt, and washer with a tab on one end of the bolt. This tab slides into the lip on the back of the molding.

We thought this molding clip was homemade, but it turned out to be a '50s GM style. A similar clip can be fashioned in your home shop using a small square of sheet metal and a bolt.

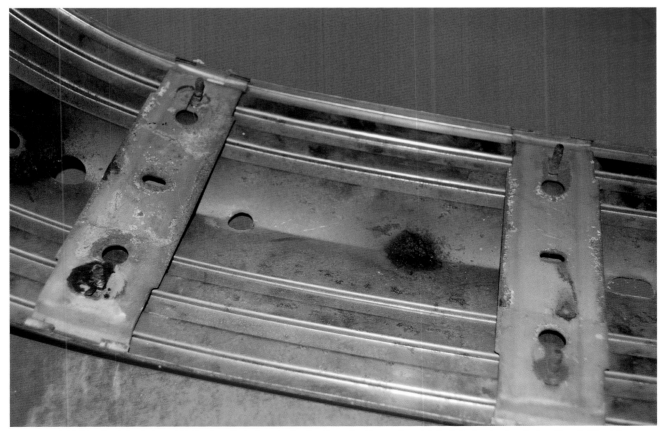

These plates hold Silver Streak hood trim on '50s Pontiacs. The bolts protruding from the underside pass through holes in the hood and are fastened by nuts. The plates are held on by crimps at each end.

If you want to reuse the original Silver Streak attaching plates with your restored moldings, you can uncrimp the plate at each end using this type of pliers. We bought pliers at Harbor Freight for a few bucks.

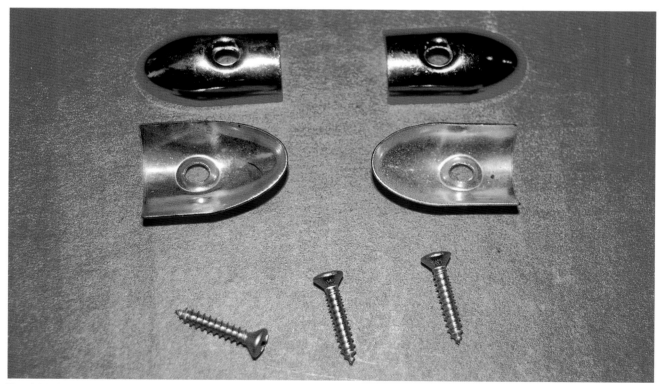

These bright-finished end caps are used to attach moldings to convertible top bows. The concave, bullet-shaped caps fit over the ends of the molding to hold it, and small screws fasten the end caps in place.

If the molding is held to the body with snap-in-place plastic clips, it will have to be carefully pried off without hurting the sheet metal or finish. A small padded screwdriver or a flat putty knife wrapped in masking tape might do the trick. This is where Eastwood's plastic pry tool set would really come in handy.

When spring-V clips are used to hold trim on, strong pressure will be needed to remove the molding if you try to just pry it out. This can easily damage the holes or slots that the spring wire passes through. If possible, it is a good idea to get behind the panel and squeeze the V-shaped part of the spring wire together with pliers. Fasteners of this style are commonly used for attaching upholstered inner door panels. Some have X-shaped—rather than V-shaped—spring wire ends. Both are removed the same way.

Dirt, grease, and rust can cause problems in removing trim fasteners. You should have a collection of all types of conventional and wire brushes to clean the small bolts and various types of clips. One of our favorite tools is an old "gnarly brush," which does a great job loosening the worst crud. Spraying the fasteners with WD-40 or PB Blaster will help.

ASSESSING THE CONDITION OF ORIGINAL TRIM

Is the bright metal trim you've removed from your car restorable? And, considering the investment of time and money, is it really worth restoring? These are two questions to ask yourself before going forward.

Whether a piece *can* be restored is a technical question. The answer depends on the condition of the piece and whether there are products and techniques that can be used to restore it. If the original trim is *serviceable*, it can be reused "as is." This is a pretty rare situation. If the trim is *salvageable*, it can be restored. In both of these cases, your restoration will move along faster, most likely cost less, and possibly be better than if you substituted reproduction parts. There is nothing like fixing a car with original parts.

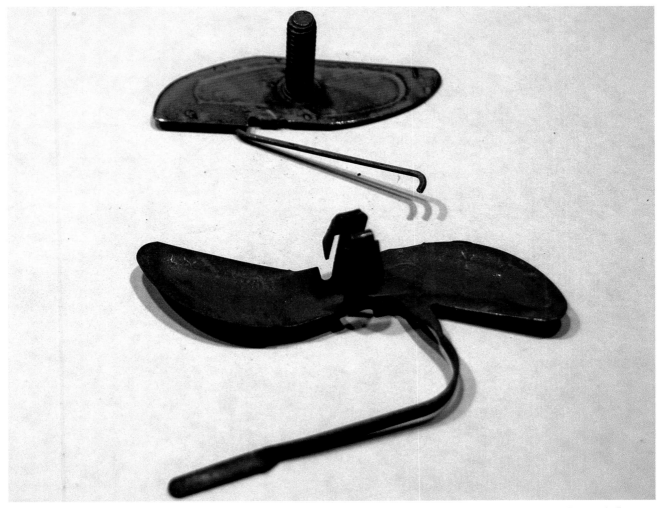

This was a common type of molding clip. The thin spring arm clips under the lip on back of the molding and then the body of the clip can be twisted to slip under the lip to secure the trim.

If the trim is *nonsalvageable*—damaged beyond the point where it can be restored—it is going to affect the cost and quality of your restoration. The piece will have to be replaced—or discarded. Replacement trim parts will carry a cost and, in some cases, may be of lesser quality. If no replacements are available, you will either have to have one fabricated—a very expensive process—or make the decision to restore the car without that piece of trim. That leaves you with either a plainer-looking vehicle or a modified car.

When an original trim piece is salvageable, you have to estimate how much it will cost to restore it and whether it's worth putting that much into the car. Let's say you're restoring a plain-Jane, early '50s Plymouth sedan and you find that a trim item is beyond restoration by buffing, polishing, or rechroming it. You may determine that painting the trim instead of plating it can be done much cheaper and doesn't hurt the car's value.

In a second scenario, you may be restoring a '55 Chevy and discover that an original piece of bright metal trim is beyond repair. No problem; you can order a reproduction piece right out of a catalog. When the car is done, it will be hard or impossible to tell the difference.

In a third scenario, you may be restoring a Duesenberg that's missing a trim piece. This valuable classic is definitely worth restoring to full factory specs, but no reproduction parts are offered. In this case, it will be worth having a replacement part fabricated.

Nonsalvageable Trim

While most bright metal auto trim can be restored by experts like Matt Kokolis of Glassworks or Mike Freund of Classics Plus, you cannot reverse *every* type of damage that the "tinsel" on a classic car endures! The ability to repair trim is determined by a number of factors like the type of damage, the extent of the damage, and the design of the piece itself.

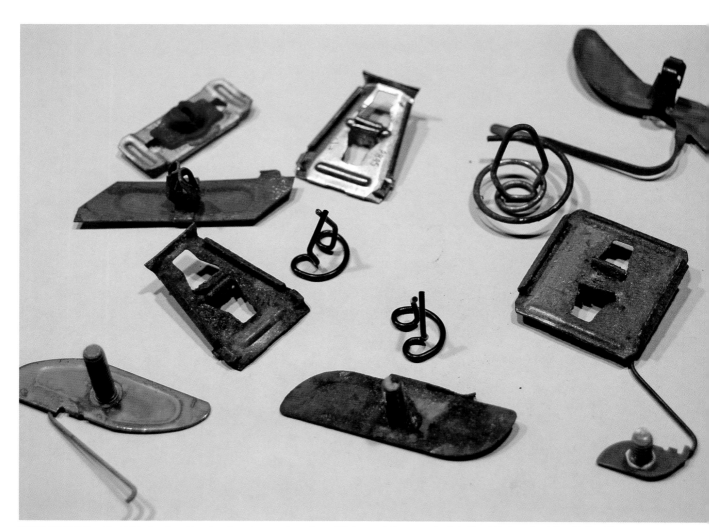

Certain clip designs were used for decades, although part numbers may have changed. Today, most clips are made of plastic, which doesn't rust like old clips did.

When a clip is rusty, the hardware may spin when you try to remove it. By using a socket wrench on one side and needle-nose or vise-grip pliers to hold the fastener on the other side, you can usually remove it.

This tight-fitting '57 MG Magnette hood molding requires use of a putty knife with thin blade. Slide it under the molding to pry the attaching clips from the holes in the hood. Be sure to protect the finish with a pad.

A flat bladed putty knife can also be used to remove loose-fitting moldings, like this 1948 Pontiac lower body sill molding. Even in this case, use plenty of padding, as it's very easy to ruin paint with such a tool.

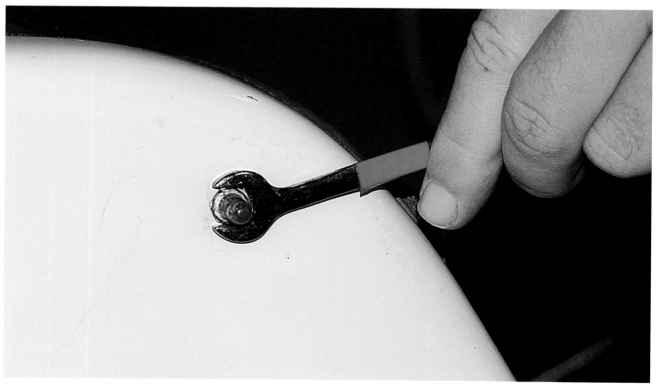

Sometimes convertibles and roadsters have special shiny hardware. This attaching stud on a 1954 MG TF is designed to hold the tonneau cover in place. It can be removed with a small open-end wrench.

Tarnishing, small dents and creases, dimples, dings, minor bends, scratches, and light oxidation can all probably be dealt with via standard auto trim restoration techniques. At Glassworks, Matt Kokolis buys up all of the spare Corvette hardtop trim he can in almost any condition. "Just about everything is fixable these days," he told us. "And we can usually find a use for most spare parts."

Heavy collision damage and heavy rust damage—like you see on cars sitting in fields and salvage yards—are the types of deterioration most likely to be irreversible. There is not a lot that can be done when a trim part is twisted and broken by the force of an impact. In the case of heavy rust, the value of a part depends on whether the corrosion is on the surface of the metal or whether it has eaten holes through the piece. If there is no rust-through, it may be possible to smooth and fill the surface and paint or powder coat the part

to make it look good. That way, it can at least be used on a Resto-Mod, custom, or hot rod.

The design of a molding, badge, shield, or other trim piece can play into its likelihood of being salvageable. Let's say the part has light collision damage. If it originally had a totally smooth surface—especially a smooth, flat surface—a talented metalworker can probably restore its original appearance. However, if it has a design with beading, compound curves, and sculpturing, it is most likely impossible to make it look new again.

When a part is nonsalvageable and no reproduction is available, finding a salvageable used part is the best option. Hobby publications like *Old Cars Weekly, Hemmings Motor News,* and *Auto Trader Classic Cars & Parts* carry ads from salvage yards around the country that break up old cars and sell the parts from them through the mail.

A hook tool, like this dental pick with a holed end, can be carefully worked under a windshield molding to pull on it to loosen it. Work slow and carefully, since bright metal moldings are thin and easy to dimple.

Salvageable Trim

If the trim on your collector vehicle is salvageable, you're fortunate. This can save you a lot of money and hassles. It may still pay to put the trim through the complete restoration process, but at least you'll have a good starting point for your project.

To repair and buff the trim, you will have to remove it. Start by taking photos that you can refer to for proper placement when reinstalling the bright stuff later on. A digital camera works best. The camera's memory card can hold lots of photos, so take enough to give you multiple views of each trim piece and be sure to take pictures of how it's attached to the car.

Each piece of trim, as well as each clip or fastener, should be tagged as well as photographed. At discount department stores you can buy tie-on tags in white and different day-glow colors. You may want to use one color for parts from the right-hand side of the car and the other color for left-hand parts.

When original trim parts from your car can't be salvaged, there are a variety of ways to find replacements—at least for many cars. Classified ads in hobby publications and club magazines often offer trim. In fact, the one-marque club magazines are usually an excellent source of parts since they go out to people interested in the same type of car.

Today, online auctions provide another source of vintage car parts. We have had mixed results when buying online. Some sellers do a good job properly identifying their inventory, but many seem to simply guess at what cars a part might fit. Other online sellers write up aftermarket parts as if they were new old stock factory parts. We have purchased rare parts online—and sometimes at bargain prices—but we have learned to look very closely at the photos that sellers post and to ask questions by email.

Every piece of bright trim on a car is made to be installed in production and removed for repairs. This '36 Pontiac Silver Streak piece is designed with an interlocking seam that allows it to be removed in sections.

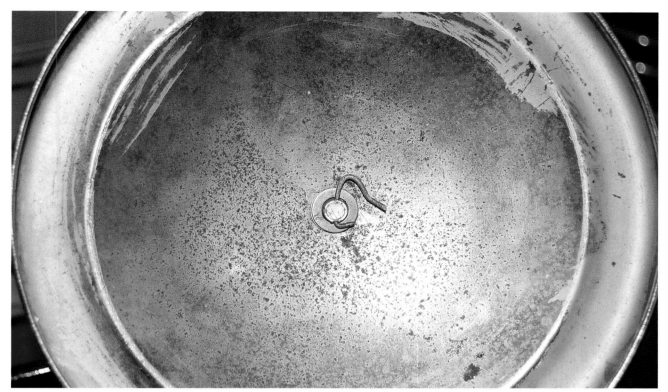

Stud with washer and cotter key secure an emblem to the outside of this MG hubcap. Some trim restorers clean up backs of repaired pieces and some do not.

Instead of fabric padding, a plastic body filler spatula can be used to protect paint when removing chrome with a putty knife. Pick the largest spatula so your paint gets the most protection.

Naturally, salvageable trim is available from salvage yards and more and more of these businesses are setting up mail order operations. When ordering replacement trim from a salvage yard, be sure to send a photo of your old piece so that you'll be sure that you get an exact match. Also be fussy about having the parts securely packaged for damage-free shipping.

Cleaning and Preparing Trim for Restoration

Use Eastwood's Metal Wash—a water-based parts cleaner—to clean trim prior to its restoration. Metal Wash removes oily preservatives, contaminants, and grease. It contains corrosion inhibitors that prevent flash rust for up to three weeks. The powder mixes with water, making up to 10 gallons of cleaner.

Apply the Metal Wash, working it into dirt on the front and back of the part. The backs of bright moldings and other trim collect crud, mudlike dirt, carwash residue, and rust. Parts that you buy from salvage yards or other hobbyists may have been off the car awhile and tend to be even dirtier. Hubcaps will have a layer of gray brake dust. Wear a facemask when cleaning them and be careful not to breathe in the asbestos-laden dust!

Use a 3M scuff pad to get the back sides of trim clean, but *do not* scuff the bright side. Rinse the scrubbed part with clean water and dry it with a clean, soft rag to avoid scratching the surface. Blow it dry with compressed air, removing any wash solution in hidden areas like molding lips and hubcap attaching tangs.

Most hubcaps, and possibly a few other parts, were factory finished with "flash chrome" over stainless steel. This has to be removed before you repair and polish the piece. Fill a 5-gallon tub with 3 gallons of water and immerse the hubcap or part. Add a half gallon of muriatic acid (used in swimming pools). Swirl the mixture and let the part soak for 10 to 15 minutes, checking periodically three or four times.

When you see a dull, rainbowlike appearance on the surface of the part, the flash chrome is gone. Next, pour a half pound of baking soda into the tub to neutralize the acid. When it stops bubbling, remove the part and safely discard the neutralized mixture. Fill the tub with clean water to rinse the part off and dry it with air and a soft towel.

Inspect the cleaned part closely under light. Pinpoint areas that need repair with a black marker pen. Another way to pick out problem areas is to wet sand it with 400-grit paper on a rubber sanding block. Any dent or depression that the sandpaper doesn't hit will remain shiny and can be marked for repair.

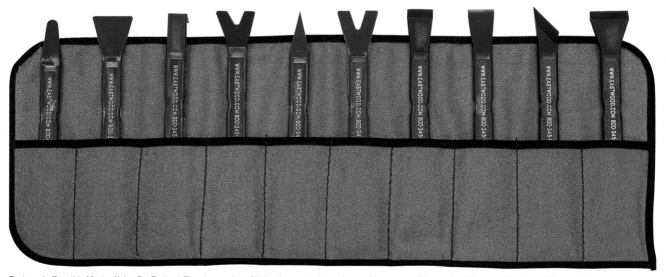

Eastwood offers this Master Nylon Pry Tool set. The strong, glass-filled nylon pry tools can be used to remove all types of moldings and hardware. They work better than a putty knife and are gentler on your car

Chapter 5
Metalworking Techniques

Metalworking is the process of working with metals to shape or form parts, assemblies, or structures. The term covers everything from jewelry making to bridge building. In restoring bright metal auto trim, we will be dealing with metals that were "worked" when the automaker made the part, so we'll actually be doing "metal reworking." The challenge will be bringing parts made long ago back to their original shape.

We can work metal because it is malleable and ductile. These properties allow us to shape it using tools and machines. In repairing auto trim, we'll be using sheetmetal shaping techniques like hammering, bending, pressing, and wheeling.

To restore the shape of the car parts, we'll use hammers, files, chisels, punches, sandbags, slapping hammers, body dollies, wood forms, picks, and other items. "Whatever it takes," says Steve Hamilton of Hamilton Classics.

Steve's well-organized restoration shop, located next to his home in Fond du Lac, Wisconsin, houses countless shaping tools he bought or made himself. He showed us drawers full of rounded chisels and unique wooden "dies" that he has made for shaping auto trim parts. Steve does show-winning, authentic restorations of '57 Chevys and only restores trim for cars he's doing. He has a deep interest in metalworking and attends www.metalmeet.com each October.

Steve Hamilton of Hamilton Classics holds three of his modified chisels. He buys the tools at garage sales or swap meets for a few dollars and grinds and polishes them to suit his needs.

A well-organized Steve Hamilton reaches into one of the drawers in a toolbox in his shop to get one of the wooden "dies" he has made over the years to help him shape sheet metal and bright metal trim.

Mike Freund, of Classics Plus Ltd., a second Fond du Lac shop, restores bright metal auto trim as a sideline to his car, truck, and steering wheel restoration services. The first thing Mike does is to inspect the piece and determine if it's worth doing. "Let's say someone gives me a front fender spear for a '55 Chevy and it has 10–12 dings," says Freund. "What we might try to do is find them a better piece we can buy and restore for $40—$50 to save the customer money."

WHEN METAL CAN'T BE WORKED

Though Freund tries to help customers, you can't replace every piece of trim on a car. GM made a lot of 1955 Chevys, but far fewer 1955 Hudsons were built. Sometimes an original piece may have been soldered, brazed, or welded to save it. Freund takes such work to "Cowboy Bob" Norris at Grade A Welding Co., across the street from Classics Plus. Norris says Mike doesn't bring him many pieces to repair, but Terry Meetz of Custom Plating Service, in Brillion, Wisconsin, says that he deals in metal repair "12 hours a day five days per week."

According to Meetz, the pits on the back of a piece concern him the most. "If it's pitted on the back, it will

This toolbox drawer at Hamilton Classics in Fond du Lac, Wisconsin, is loaded with homemade metal-shaping tools like rounded chisels, rounded punches, and shaped pieces of wood.

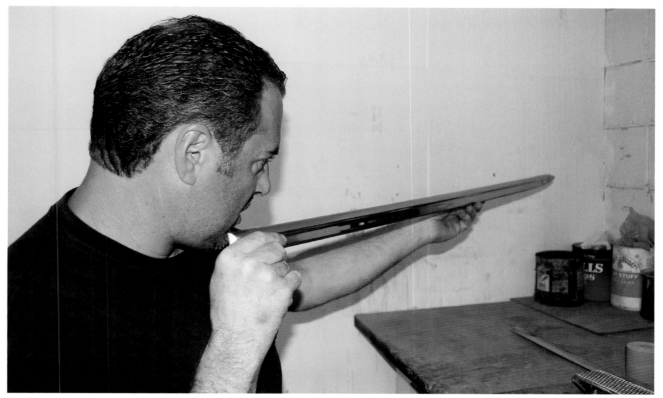

Mike Freund of Classics Plus, Ltd., in North Fond du Lac, Wisconsin, sights down a 1956 Chevy front fender spear looking for flaws in the trim piece. If he spots dings or bends, he'll hammer the metal straight.

be pitted on the front, even if it doesn't look bad," he says. "When you polish it, you might find rust-through, and that's a problem." Terry says that weather, salt, and moisture cause a lot of the pitting seen on the back of pieces. "Where the car was waxed, there will be less pitting showing, but people didn't wax the backs of the trim, so a lot of times the backs are the worst."

If a piece is heavily pitted, Terry asks, "Can we fix it and how?" His big concern is what he calls dead metal. "If you poke with an ice pick and it goes through, the part may not be fixable," says Meetz. "You get that once in a while."

Tools and equipment are a big part of satisfactorily repairing automotive trim. The proper hand tools and the right machines will make it easier to do the job and will get you better results.

Hammering

Hammering is such an important part of bright metal auto trim restoration that Matt Kokolis of Glassworks: The Hardtop Shop is making an automatic hammering machine to hammer stainless trim. We saw his prototype.

Small, lightweight hammers are used to straighten trim and tap out dings. Mike Freund's largest just hangs over a standard 8½x11 sheet of paper and the smallest takes up half the paper. Freund says he bought his hammers from a swap meet vendor.

Mike Freund does a lot of restoration work that involves straightening and refinishing metal. His projects run from classic cars to vintage gas pumps.

Terry Meetz, owner of Custom Plating Specialists in Brillion, Wisconsin, said that this old car part with heavy pitting on the back will probably have pitting on the front that will be cut through when buffing it.

Terry Meetz buffs a piece of trim behind a sturdy metal shield that lowers on a chain. The shield prevents objects or particles thrown by the wheel from striking the operator's face or chest.

Matt Kokolis, of Glassworks: The Hardtop Shop in Crescent, Pennsylvania, designed this trim hammering machine. He expects to have it perfected and on the market very soon.

Eastwood sells a small repousse hammer and trim anvil. They come separate or in a kit. Eastwood also offers a mini anvil and hammer. The mini has blunt-chisel head that can get inside the U-shaped rear lip of trim moldings.

Metal trim is straightened by lightly tapping out dings. The trim needs to be supported on a block of wood, anvil, or sandbag. Steve Hamilton of Hamilton Classics says the rule is "No hard on hard or soft on soft." For example, when using a hard tool like a hammer, use a soft support like a sandbag.

Work from the back, tapping lightly. Use a tap-in-a-circle technique. Start with a large circle on the outer edge of the ding and keep shrinking the size of the circle as you tap it out. Flip the trim over and file the surface. Usually, a small pinhead dent will remain. Mark it on the back, then tap lightly right on the mark.

The outer surface may look very rough half-way through the process. Don't give up. Filing, sanding, and buffing can transform the piece.

Shaping

"After removing dings, I take really fine, fine files and lightly go across the surface to level it," says Freund. "I make half a dozen passes. If there's still a ding, I'll bring that up from the back to avoid filing the trim too thin. You won't know how thin it is until you polish. If it's too thin, it'll warp."

Lips, bends, creases, and ridges in trim must be returned to their original shapes. Rounded chisels and punches and wood forms are handy for shaping. Steve Hamilton buys old rusty tools "for almost nothing." He cleans, grinds, and

Mike Freund said he picked up these three hammers from a swap meet vendor. These are all of the same basic design with different-size handles and heads. That's a standard sheet of paper, for size reference.

These hammers from Mike Freund's toolbox at Classic Plus, Ltd., all have different-style working heads: (Left) wedge style; (center) thin head for shaping edges of trim lip; (right) bullet-shaped brass head.

Mike Freund brings dings up using a "double hammer" technique. He hammers from the back of a molding, against a sandbag sitting on a rubber mat. Trying to file the dings away could cut through the trim.

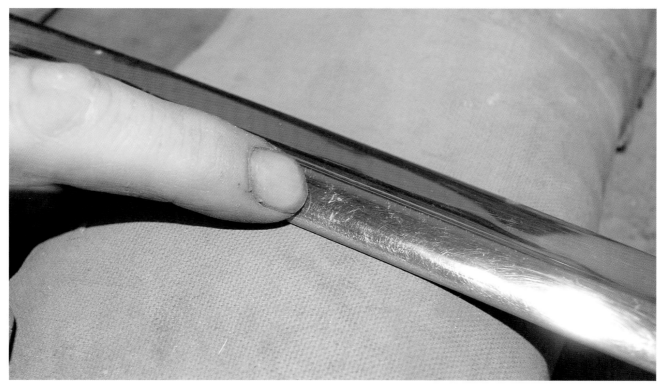

After hammering it as straight as possible, Mike Freund flipped this Chevrolet molding over and pointed to a single remaining pinpoint in the metal. This is what commonly occurs.

Freund has flipped the molding over once again and will lightly tap down the single small highpoint. This time, he'll tap directly on the pinpoint "dimple."

polishes them for shaping use. Such tools must be clean, smooth, and polished or they will transfer imperfections on their contact surface to the trim piece.

A chisel about ½-inch wide can tap dings out of creases in concave or convex trim pieces (like grille bars). Place the piece over a smooth block of wood. Tap on one end of the crease, then the other. Work the depression smooth from its outer edges inward. Then, repeat with a smaller-width chisel, tapping lightly to give the creased area a crisp line like it originally had.

Hamilton makes brackets to hold moldings in vises using a plate just wide enough to slip into the lips on the rear of the molding. He welds a second plate to the center of the first at 90 degrees. He slips the molding onto the first plate and clamps the other in his vise. (An alternative is taping the molding to your support.)

Steve removes small dings by clamping an ice pick in his vise with the point facing up. He sets the back of the molding, where the ding is, on the tip of the ice pick and taps down on top of the piece with the palm of his hand.

Edging

It's best to straighten outer edges of trim first, rather than the "body." When you do edges first, you are focusing on the section that contacts the car's paint and relieving stress in the molding so that its body can move as it's restored.

Use a ½ to 1-inch wide chisel with its blade rounded to match the corner edge of the molding. Lightly tap out the edges along their length. The goal is to get them level and straight. Tap with the piece on a 1x4-inch block. Have an assistant hold the part at different angles to help you to tap in the right spots.

Once you've filed the surface near the edge and have it straight, check to make sure you have room to work the back side, near its edge. Focus on the area covered by the lip on the back of the molding. Finish tapping out irregularities with a tacking hammer like upholsterers use.

Check the edge for highs or dips. As the molding is tightened to the car body, such irregularities will put pressure on the finish and crack the paint. To fix a dip, tape across the surface of the molding to make a "plum line." Put the taped side against your wooden block or anvil and use a squared hammer to bring the dip down to your plum line. On a high point, do the opposite.

A vise is another handy device for straightening molding edges on flat moldings. Tape and pad the vise jaws or purchase commercial jaw pads from companies like Eastwood. Put the molding in the vise and use a wide-blade chisel to pry up on the edge until it has a uniform height along the length of the

trim. While you are prying, hold the other end of the piece with your hand.

Repair Methods

You've heard of the metals titanium and uranium, but did you ever hear of *unobtainium*? We bought a '57 Buick and thought the rusty bumper ends would be replaceable. These were prone to rusting because the exhaust pipes passed through them. The next month a set of replated bumper ends were in *Hemmings* for $700. "Too high," we said. Now, we'd buy as many sets as we could get for $700. As a friend of ours likes to say, "That part is made of 'unobtainium.'"

It's the same with some moldings, gravel shields, nameplates, hubcaps, and other trim parts. They must be made of unobtainium, because the only way to replace them is to do major repairs to originals or *make* reproductions. This is where the talents and creativity of restorers come into play.

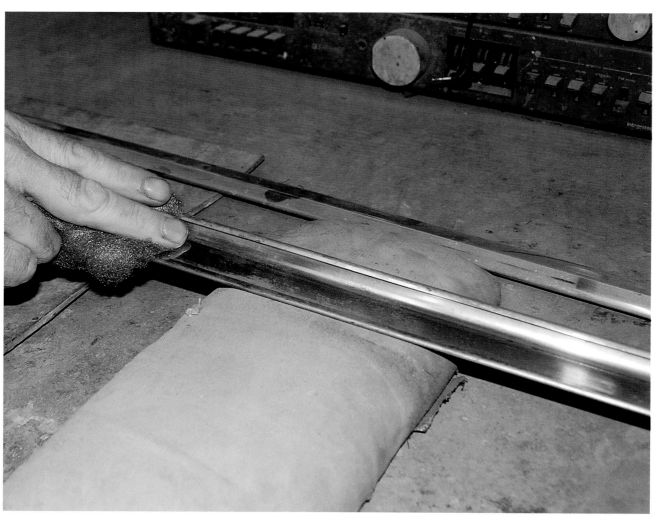

Mike Freund likes to polish the surface of the metal with 00 steel wool as he gets near the end of the job. The steel wool will clean the stainless up and tends to highlight any minor imperfections that remain.

Mike files across the piece and is careful to make no more than a half dozen strokes. This keeps him from removing too much metal. Also, if it's been fixed before, be careful not to overdo it.

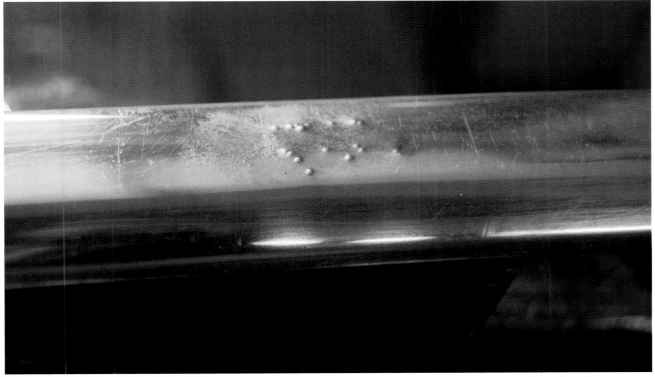

Don't panic. Steve Hamilton put the raised spots into this molding so he could demonstrate using a bumping or slapping spoon to bring them down and make the surface smooth again.

When used in the way Steve Hamilton is working, slapping spoons spread the force of a blow over a wide area. As the spoon and finger blur here indicate, Hamilton taps the spoon onto the raised bumps to smooth them flat. They can also be used like a dolly or as a prying or driving tool.

This illustrates the use of a slapping spoon and metal plate of the proper size and shape to form the edges ("lips") of a molding. Steve Hamilton says practicing on scrap metal is a way to learn use of a spoon.

Restorer Steve Hamilton made this bracket that slides into the lips on the back of a molding. Then, the plate welded to it perpendicularly can be clamped into a vise. This is a better way to hold a piece than taping it.

We're not saying that no one ever fabricated a reproduction part for a specific car, but this isn't how most hobbyists do it. Unless you find that the chrome strip on your storm windows or your flagpole is an exact match for the damaged one on your Duesenberg, you are probably going to try to *repair* the original so that it can be refinished to look like new. This involves straightening the piece, repairing rips and tears, and patching rust holes. Soldering and welding are some of the skills you'll be using.

Before you can use such methods to repair the damage, the part must be cleaned, as described in Chapter 4. The next step is to inspect it carefully and use an indelible marker to indicate where repairs are required. Then, use a bumping dolly to straighten the torn section and return the bent metal to close-to-original shape. The damaged area should have only a small gap when it is shaped back to its original form.

Soldering

Repairing auto trim with solder differs from soldering wires in an old radio. The solder used is lead body filler—traditionally a 30 percent tin/70 percent lead alloy. Lead solder is safe, but lead dust in the air isn't, so when shaping the solder, file it by hand and wear a respirator or use the lead-free copper/zinc alloy solders that companies like Eastwood sell.

Lead (lead-free) body solder is popular in the restoration of classic cars. It's simple to use, but requires certain skills to do it well. The basic materials like the lead and flux or "tinning butter" are available in kits or individually. You will need paddles, paddle lube, acid brushes, body files, and a torch.

The area on the trim piece where the lead is going to be applied has to be cleaned of all paint, corrosion, dirt, and grease. A sanding disc or wire brush will get the metal clean and bright. You can then apply the lead (lead-free) filler.

Heat the surface with a torch to keep it warm while the lead is put on. The end of the lead stick is heated, too. The solder sticks to the surface and you then twist the stick off. Lead is continually added until there is enough to fill the damaged area. Overheating a panel causes warping, so allow everything to cool occasionally. Learning to use just enough heat to get the job done is important.

Once it's on the panel, the solder must be kept warm enough to remain plastic. Use flat or round wooden paddles to shape it. Dip the paddles in tallow or beeswax to keep the lead from sticking. The hot lead can be smoothed very close to its final shape. After it cools by itself, without quenching, use a brush and water to clean things up.

Welding

A MIG welder is handy for repairing trim. Get a good one, gloves, an apron, and a self-darkening helmet. Keep a ¼- to ⅜-inch stick-out (electrode extension from tip). The thinner the piece, the thinner the wire. Charts on the machine will give recommendations.

Use stainless-steel wires for stainless-steel trim, aluminum wires for aluminum, etc. Use argon shielding gas for aluminum. For stainless steel use a triple-mix of helium + argon + carbon dioxide.

For best bead control, direct the wire at the leading edge of the weld pool. Match your contact tube, gun liner, and drive rolls to wire size. Keep gun liners, drive rolls, and nozzles clean. Weld with the gun straight. Use two hands to steady it. Keep hub tension and drive roll pressure tight enough to feed wire without overtightening. Keep wire clean and dry. Put the welder's power source button on the DCEP setting.

A drag or pull gun technique gives you more penetration and a narrower bead. A push gun technique gives you less penetration and a wider bead. Refer to www.millerwelds.com/education/tech_tips/MIG_tips/ for proper adjustments.

Steve Hamilton thought of using an ice pick to lift very small low spots out of a molding and found it to work well. Lock the ice pick upright and put very light downward pressure on the trim to work the low spots out.

When using the ice pick method, pressure can also be applied via light tapping with a soft hammer.

When filling steel using a welder, get it glowing red, then back off for a second. While the weld is glowing, touch the trigger. Keep the piece glowing without continuously holding the trigger down. This lets the weld cool slightly, but still melt. It also prevents burn-through.

On a wide flat rocker panel molding, use a damp rag to cool the weld every quarter inch. This prevents warping. You should place a damp rag under a cracked or torn area while welding it.

After weld cools, grind it to a smooth finish. Use a hand-held grinder with 24- to 36-grit discs. Cut the bead down to about $\frac{1}{32}$-inch above the surface. Use an Ingersoll Rand 302 angle grinder, Mirka Trim-Kut self-sharpening tool, or Eastwood flap discs. Finish by grinding with an 80-grit disc. A dual-action sander with 80-grit paper, set on grinding mode works, too. Don't grind through.

TOOLS AND EQUIPMENT

Bumping hammers, dolly blocks, and slapping spoons used in body shops are handy for restoring metal trim with large, contoured areas. The procedures used for these repairs are similar to standard auto body techniques, but remember to tap lightly, rather than hammering forcefully. The skills involved in metalworking can be as old as medieval times or as new as the innovation a modern restorer developed last week.

In this example, Mike Freund is trying to illustrate how to straighten a molding with a slight bow by bridging it across two objects and applying very light pressure. Usually, he uses wooden blocks as his supports.

A variety of tools come in handy when restoring bright metal auto trim. Steve Hamilton likes to use a DA (dual-action) sander set on grinding mode to level metal rather than filing it.

Ron Covell of Covell Creative Metalworking in Freedom, California, sells modern tools like rounding-over dies that form a constant-radius curve on the edge of a panel, but also offers old-school English wheels, plus workshops and DVDs that teach age-old metalworking techniques.

Bill Politsch of Mittler Bros. Machine & Tool says his Top and Bottom Sheet Metal Finger Brake is popular for making hot rod parts and his new air-operated English wheel is in demand. Car builders like his powered bead roller, but sheetmetal brakes and tubing benders generate more revenue for him.

Bob Lorkowski of L'Cars restoration shop in Cameron, Wisconsin, has a shop full of metalworking tools, including a Magee Wire Edger, Pullmax, Pexto, and various wheels and shrinker-stretchers. Lorkowski's www.Lcars.com website has a metalworking video on it. With wheels, rollers, and metal benders, the shop makes body panels like those coachbuilders once pounded out by hand.

Steve Frisbie, of Steve's Auto Restoration in Portland, Oregon, says, "The demand for metal-fabrication tools is greater than it has been in the past. I see young and old people wanting to learn and get involved in metal shaping and lead work." Frisbie says these skills have been described as "black arts."

Carolyn Bindenagel of Roper-Whitney discovered a sheet-metal museum in Pennsylvania and found collectors that specialize in her company's Pexto tools from its Peck, Stoew & Wilcox era, 1870–1950. "They call them 'Pextonians,'" she said.

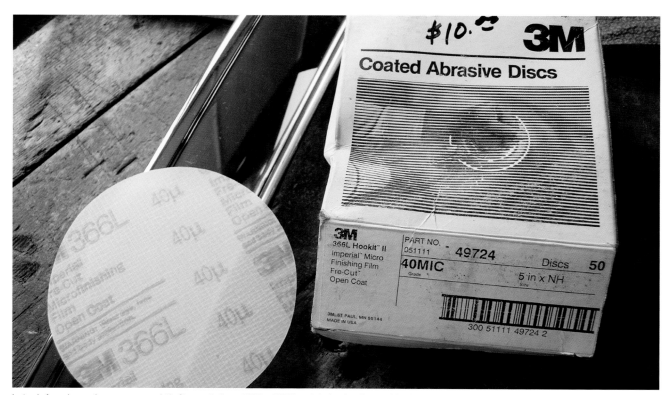

Instead of regular sandpaper or emery cloth, Steve puts these 3M No. 40724 coated abrasive discs on his DA sander and turns it into a grinder that actually "files" the surface of trim moldings flat.

Chapter 6
Refinishing Techniques

Hammering, shaping, and edging metal changes its form. Hammering flattens the metal and raises the dents, dings, and creases in it. Filing levels the surface of the metal and takes out deep scratches. Rounded-off files, wooden forming tools, ice picks, and other tools shape metal or return it to its original shape. Edging makes the rolled lips on the back of trim straight and uniform so that they can be fitted with clips needed to hold a piece to the car.

Once the metal is shaped, its surface must be refinished. In the case of bright metal, we will need to smooth it so that it regains its original sheen and luster. Metal can often be returned to this state by careful sanding and buffing. If you can get it sufficiently smooth without polishing through it or warping it, the piece can be restored. In the case of coated metal, it must be smooth before being coated. In this chapter, the focus will be on refinishing bright metal.

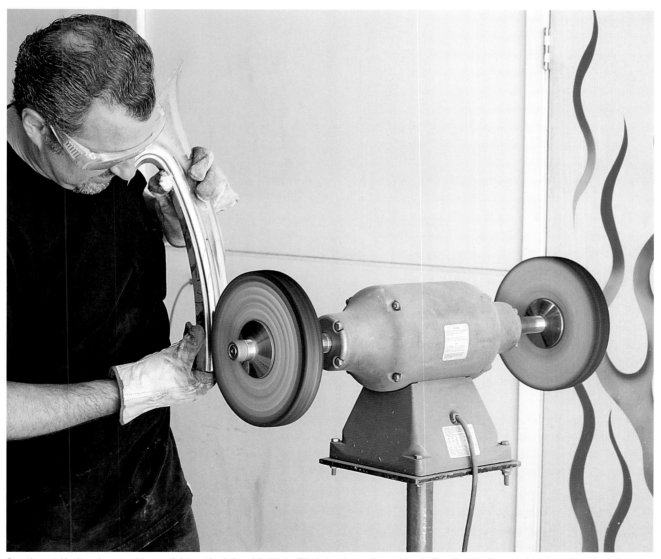

Once the metal is shaped, you need to smooth it to get back the original luster. This is done by sanding and then buffing, like Mike Freund is doing here. *Jesse Gunnell*

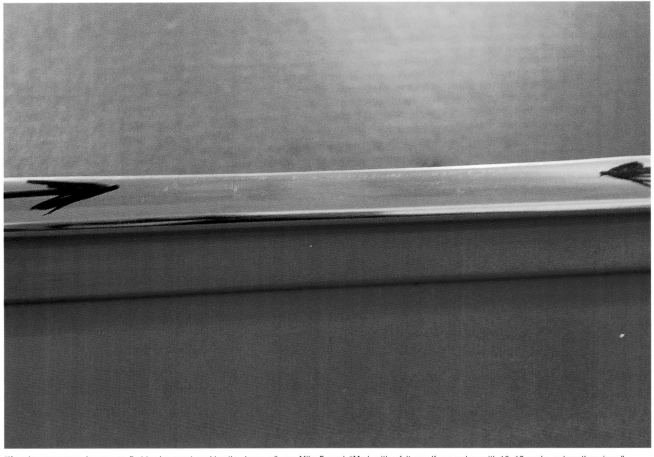

"If you're an average Joe on your first try, I suggest marking the damage," says Mike Freund. "Mark with a felt pen. If you end up with 10–12 marks, get another piece."

MARKING

Marking is a procedure in which damage to a piece being worked is sighted and then marked with a black ink marker. In visiting professional shops, we noticed that few restorers marked their work. Most sighted down the piece with their eyes, under shaded light, and then started right in.

"Well, you *can* mark," Mike Freund of Classics Plus, Ltd., told us. "I mean, if you're an average Joe making your first try at this stuff, I would suggest marking it. Mark every piece with a felt pen. If you end up with 10–12 marks, try to get another piece. That's what I've done for customers. Why charge someone $150 to fix a molding with a lot of damage, when you can buy a better one for $15 and restore it for $50?" Though Mike looks at this from a customer service angle, the home restorer can also save work by economical replacements.

If you decide to mark damage, some experts feel it's best to draw an arrow pointing in the direction of the flaw and sand in the opposite direction. Pits can be circled. The marker ink will get into even the lowest areas. Later, as you sand the marked spots, the ink from the marker will begin to disappear, first from the high spots and then from lower spots. The ink that got into the lowest point will disappear last and that will signal that the piece is smooth.

SANDING

After you have flattened the molding with a hammer, filed it level, shaped it, worked the edges, sighted flaws, and marked them, you can sand the piece. Some will recommend six sandpaper grits—80, 180, 220, 320, 400, and 600—but many pros use fewer grits to control their investments in time and materials.

"Usually, I start with 180-grit and work my way up to 240," says Mike Freund. "Then, I'll go to 320, 400, and 600. Once in a while, if I want a superfine finish, I will hit it with 1,000–1,200-grit. I've actually done that a few times."

Freund sands by hand with his paper on a plastic block that he has given a flamed paint job. He likes to set up separate blocks with each of the grits he'll be using and have them on the bench in front of him, along with rolls of each sandpaper. He also keeps a 00 steel wool pad handy. He uses this to clean areas on the trim and make low spots easier to see. "Your low spots should be worked out as much as possible from the bottom, by hammering," he says. "Don't try to sand them away or you'll get the molding so thin it'll warp when you buff it."

Steve Hamilton, of Hamilton Classics, prefers doing the initial sanding with an air-powered DA (dual-action) sander, set on grinding mode, with a 6-inch pad. Steve bought abrasive discs at swap meets for a few dollars and they work well.

Some restorers start with 80-grit DA paper, but this cuts fast. If you use it, test on scrap metal. To smooth out minor scratches you can just feel with a fingernail, go to 180-grit DA paper. The highest to go on a DA is 320- or 400-grit to sand fine scratches that would take a long time to buff out. In addition to discs on a DA, you can use flap wheels to reach certain areas or do small pieces.

These sanding tools and supplies include a Campbell Hausfeld DA sander purchased on sale at Wal-Mart; Easy Power No. 30377 1x1-inch drum sanders (50-, 80-, 120-, and 180-grits); a Norton No. 03213 20x flap disc with zirconia abrasive; and Delta No. 31-063 1x30-inch abrasive belts.

Store-bought packages of sandpaper like these work fine. Get a range of different grits.

Eastwood sells two special tools for sanding. The natural rubber Expander Wheel conforms to slightly contoured pieces and leaves a bright, smooth, uniform finish. It can be used with the company's abrasive bands, or with Scotch-Brite belts or Trizact belts of correct width and circumference length. Such belts use aluminum oxide abrasives for cutting consistency. They are self-lubricating and resist loading up. These belts produce a uniform flat surface finish.

Final sanding with the finer grits of paper should always be done by hand with the paper attached to a sanding block. The block we use at home has slots at each end with nail teeth in them to attach the paper. More modern styles, such as Freund uses, are designed for much more convenient stick-on papers.

ADVANCED METHODS
Belt Sander

A belt sander has a motor that spins an endless sandpaper belt quickly around a pair of rollers. This tool cuts quickly and removes large amounts of metal. It is for heavy-duty sanding

Mike Freund demonstrates the use of a plastic sanding board to sand across the surface in a crisscross pattern.

Mike does a lot of sanding, so he buys his paper in different-grit rolls. He keeps one roll of each grit right on the workbench in front of him and can change paper fast.

at the start of a job before switching to your DA or hand-sanding. Remember that Matt Kokolis, of Glassworks: The Hardtop Shop, likes the belt sander for production, but it's overkill in most hobby shops.

Stationary belt sanders are expensive, too. Even hand-held belt sanders are designed for pros. After using a belt sander for a while, run the belt against a neoprene block or a large old worn-out rubber car part to clean it.

Flap Wheel

A flap wheel is made of folded abrasive strips rotating on a hub. They can range from 4 to 24 inches in diameter. The hub holds the flaps together and serves as an arbor that mounts to a rotating tool. The flaps are made of felt, neoprene, buff cloth, or cardboard. The abrasives used on them include carbides, oxides, and other materials.

Flap wheels work well as a fine grinding tool. They're helpful for preparing bright metal auto trim for buffing, plating, or anodizing. Flap wheels mounted on an air-powered die grinder are good for initial sanding operations because their flexible character allows them to conform to different shapes. They also have a fanlike quality that keeps the work cooler and reduces warping.

SETUP WHEEL

Terry Meetz uses a setup wheel to buff metal at Custom Plating Services in Brillion, Wisconsin, Terry says that his employees buff 12 hours a day, five days a week, so using a setup wheel speeds production. Above his wheel is a length of sheet metal that lowers on a chain for face protection—a good idea.

Steve Hamilton uses a DA sander with a light touch so that he doesn't bite right through the trim. He likes this Blue Point air sander.

Setup wheels are made up by stacking several spiral-sewn buffs together, balancing them, and gluing them to each other. Canvas covers can be glued to the sides of the wheels. The wheels typically have end widths of ½ inch to 4 inches. They are primarily used with coarse Turkish emery or aluminum oxide cutting compounds, but can be used with gray (stainless steel) or tripoli (soft metal) compounds. With aluminum oxide abrasives glued to the face of the buff, a setup wheel can actually be used to *grind* steel and stainless-steel surfaces. (Note: See "Buffing" below for more on buffs and buffing compounds.)

An abrasive can be applied to the setup wheel with cold glue. The glue is brushed on the face of the wheel and then it is rolled in the abrasive grit. This is repeated three times. Then, allow the glue to dry for 12 hours. When making a Turkish emery grease wheel (used to prepare parts for chrome plating) hot glue is used and the wheel is dried at 105 degrees for 12 hours.

Here is the Easy Power No. 30377 1x1inch-drum sanders (50-, 80-, 120-, and 180-grits) and one of three sanding belts that comes in the Delta No. 31-063 1x30-inch abrasive belts package. *Eastwood*

This Norton No. 03213 20x flap disc fits on a hand-held auto buffing machine.

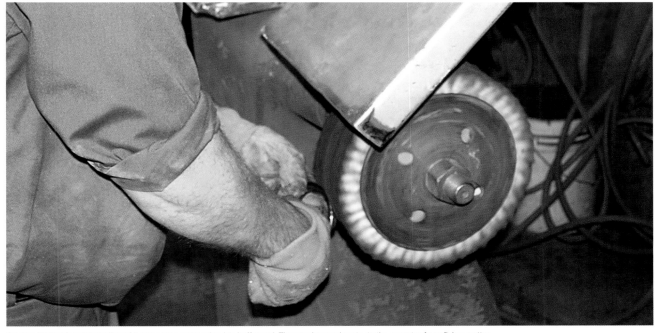

Custom Plating Specialists' Terry Meetz uses a setup wheel to buff metal. The sturdy guard protects the operator from flying matter.

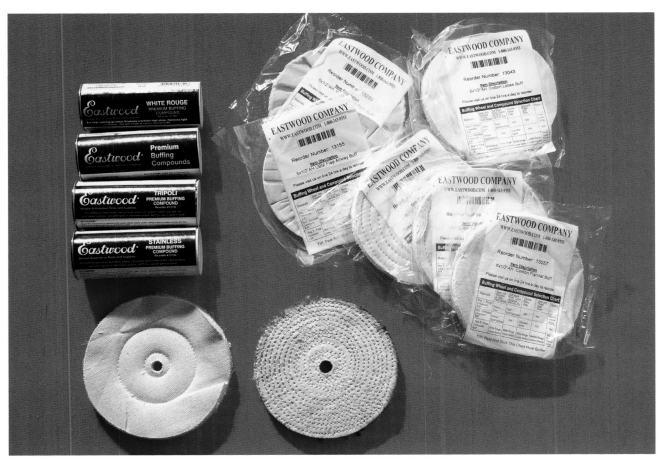

A good selection of buffs and rouges includes emery, tripoli, white buffing compound, stainless medium cut, and red jewelers' rouge.

When first finished, setup wheels can be mounted in a buffing motor and rotated by hand so that you can "crack" them with a mallet or rod to produce flexibility in the wheel. (The cracks or hits should be approximately thumb size.) The emery wheel must be greased to produce a better finish.

In industry, setup wheels are used for around two to four hours before being replaced with a new wheel while the first one is "faced off" using a carbon grinding stone. It will then be reglued and set up for another work shift. In a home shop, you can soak the wheel in water, run it against an old file, and reglue it.

You have to get used to using a setup wheel, because it can cut deep and fast and quickly ruin a piece of trim. The advantages of using one are that it will save you a lot of expense in sanding discs or sandpaper and cut the time it takes to do initial sanding on your bright metal trim.

BUFFING

The final step in restoring bright metal auto trim is buffing it to a lustrous finish. For this you will need buffs, buffing rouges, and a motor. Theoretically, an amateur could buff on a grinding wheel like Matt Kokolis suggested early in this book, but a high-speed buffing motor makes the job easier and gives much better results. Suppliers like Eastwood sell buffing motors in different price ranges.

There are various compounds and types of wheels for buffing different metals. Buffing motors come with illustrated instructions and charts that help you select the right buffs and buffing compounds. Buffs are made of cloth sewn together and the tighter the stitching, the harder and more aggressive the buff will be. A hard metal like stainless requires more aggressive buffs for initial buffing.

The sisal buff is the classic style used for stainless steel. It has spiral-sewn construction and is made of woven-rope

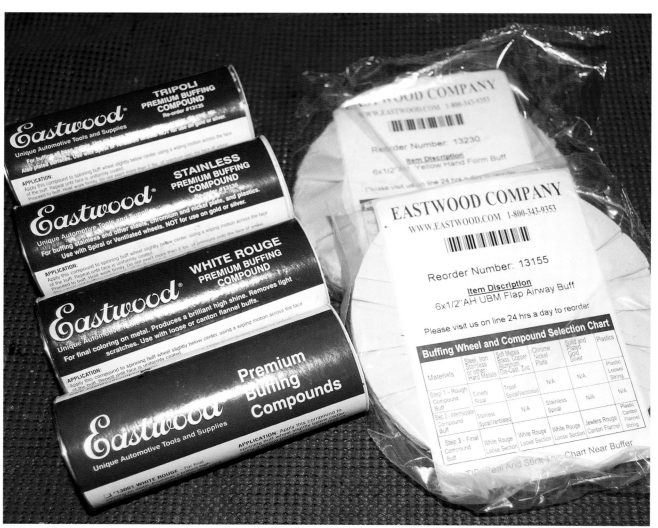

The rouges and buffs that Eastwood sells have charts on the packaging to tell you which rouges to use with specific buffs.

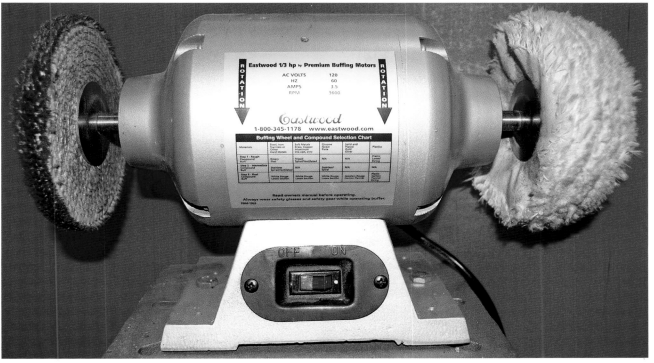

If you visit Eastwood's factory store at its headquarters in Pottstown, Pennsylvania, you will see a variety of different horsepower buffing motors amd pedestals to mount them on, as well as an assortment of buffs and buffing compounds. *Eastwood*

fiber covered with cotton cloth. A variation is the red treated sisal buff, which gives a faster cut and lasts longer. As you get to final buffing on stainless, you'll switch to one of several looser-sewn buffs used for polishing the metal after it's been smoothed down by the sisal buff.

As far as buffing rouges go, an emery compound can be used to do aggressive fast cutting on stainless steel in the initial stage of buffing it. A light to medium gray stainless compound is good for medium cutting on stainless. It can be used on a sisal or ventilated buff. The ventilated buff has pleated, biased cloth to keep the piece being worked on cooler and prevent streaking the compound. White rouge is used in the final stage to remove any light scratches left by the stainless compound. It works best on soft loose sections or canton flannel buffs that cut light and give a higher degree of shine to the stainless.

Tripoli is a midrange buffing compound that is ideal for soft metals like aluminum, pot metal, and brass. White rouge compound removes the scratches left after a hard metal is buffed with stainless emery or a soft metal is buffed with tripoli. Buffing with jeweler's rouge can follow after stainless steel or aluminum are buffed with white rouge. Of course, this compound also works well on fine metals like gold and silver as well as on plated metals.

Safety and buffer location are things to think about before spinning a wheel. The buffing motor runs at 3,600 rpm. It can shoot a part across the room so fast you'll think a slingshot dragster went by. Wear your face shield and heavy leather gloves. The gloves will protect you from the wheel

For safe, comfortable buffing, you'll want a pedestal to mount your buffing motor on. *Eastwood*

Eye protection and gloves are absolute musts for safe buffing. A respirator is also a good idea. *Eastwood*

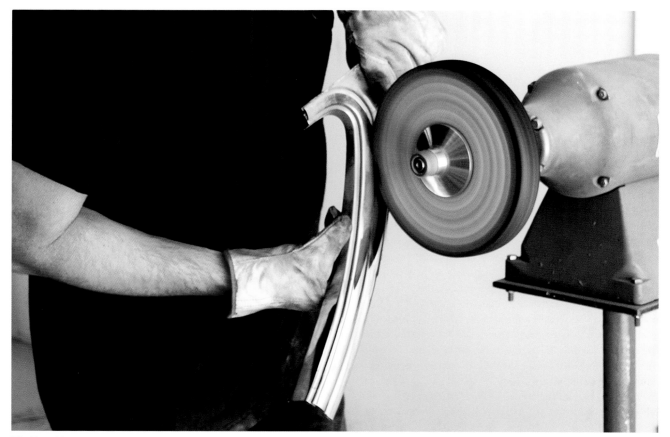

Mike Freund demonstrates how you should let the wheel run off the edge of your part when buffing.

While buffing, every few minutes, hold the bar of rouge against the lower part of the buffing wheel.

and heat. The parts being buffed get really hot. Don't wear jewelry, and tuck in any loose clothing.

When you buff, you apply buffing compounds to a rapidly spinning wheel. Some of the abrasives are going to wind up in the air, on your clothes, or on whatever is behind the buffing motor. So, wear a facemask or respirator and a shop apron. We put a yellow streak on the wall behind the buffing wheel the first time we used it. Now, we keep a big piece of cardboard against the wall.

The proper way to buff a piece is to let the wheel run off the edge of the part. Work on the lower portion of the wheel, just below its center axis. Apply the stainless-steel buffing compound to the wheel sparingly. You can take the compound in your gloved hand and carefully rub it on the spinning wheel.

While buffing the piece, avoid using too much pressure. You will buff in stages, sometimes changing wheels and compounds. If you have an extra pair of clean, heavy leather gloves, use them. This will keep the new wheel from getting the old compound on it. If you work skillfully, you can buff stainless-steel parts to the point where they have the luster and sheen of a piece of chrome.

Stainless Steel

On stainless steel, start with a sisal buff, which cuts aggressively and fast. You can also use a red treated sisal buff that is impregnated with a chemical that makes it even more aggressive. Both are suitable for use with stainless-steel emery or greaseless compounds. For coarse work, you can also use a spiral-sewn buff with stainless-steel emery. Later, you might want to use a cotton ventilated buff with stainless steel or white rouge for less aggressive buffing. Then, a loose section buff can be used with white rouge or jeweler's rouge to create a high-shine on the nearly finished piece. The loose section buff will also be able to get into hard-to-reach areas. As a final step, to get a brilliant finish, you can use an extrasoft 100 percent cotton canton flannel wheel with white or jeweler's rouge.

Aluminum

On aluminum, start with a spiral-sewn buff using tripoli compound. Then go to a ventilated buff with tripoli before switching to a second one to use with white rouge for less fine polishing. Then, a loose section buff can be used with white rouge and jeweler's rouge to create a high shine on the nearly finished piece and get into hard-to-reach areas. For your final brilliance, go to a canton flannel wheel with white or jeweler's rouge.

Brass and Copper

On soft brass or copper, the process is the same as for aluminum. With skilled use of the softer compounds and looser buffs, you can really get brass and copper to look great. Many brass parts are used on imported vehicles, such as British sports cars, and giving them a brilliant shine is very rewarding.

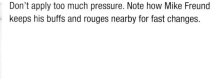
Don't apply too much pressure. Note how Mike Freund keeps his buffs and rouges nearby for fast changes.

Buffing restores the luster of metal, as you can see by the recently buffed molding on the bottom.

This minibuff kit is designed to help the restorer get into tight places. *Eastwood*

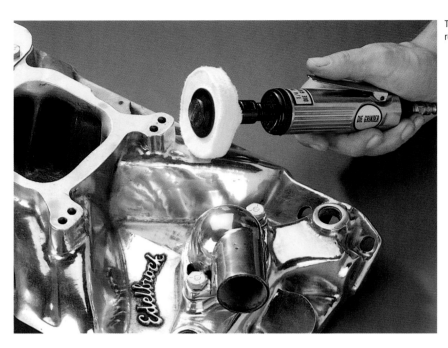

This 3-inch buff fits on a mini–die grinder and helps restorers polish small areas. *Eastwood*

Eastwood's No. 13147 five-piece minibuff kit includes large cone, ball, bullet, pointed, and tree-style buffs with ¼-inch shanks. *Eastwood*

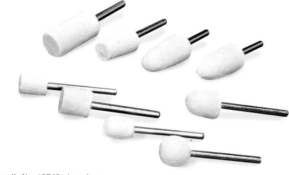

Eastwood's No. 10743 nine-piece mini–buff kit includes small cone, ball, bullet, pointed, and tree-style buffs with 1/8-inch shanks for use with a Dremel tool. *Eastwood photo*

10 TIPS FOR BUFFING

1. If you plan to go into business buffing, get a custom-made buffing system sold by companies like C. F. Global Products.
2. Sewing gives buffs their stiffness. A ⅛ spiral sewn has ⅛ inch between the stitching and is stiffer than a ⅜ spiral sewn with ⅜ inch between the stitching.
3. As buffs wear, their diameter shrinks and this reduces the surface area of the circumference. So, a newer buff always works better.
4. You need at least 7,000 feet of buffing surface per minute to buff stainless; this equates to a minimum buff wheel diameter of 8 inches.
5. Remove your compound from the cardboard container and apply it by holding the bar against the wheel at the lower portion of the front of the buff.
6. While buffing, apply more compound for about three seconds every half minute to a minute.
7. Use only one compound with each wheel. If you want to apply two types of compounds using the same type of wheel, get two wheels of that type.
8. Since some compounds look the same, do not mix them up. Return them to their original cardboard tube or box or store in labeled sandwich bags.
9. You may want to use large electrical ties to hold long pieces on a board while you buff them. Later, you can buff the small areas left by the ties.
10. Suppliers like Eastwood sell minibuffs, soft flap wheels, and fine-weave cotton buffs for reaching hard-to-get-at areas and going in tight spaces.

Chapter 7
Restoring Other Types of Metal Trim

So far, we've covered restoring stainless steel, aluminum, brass, and copper through hand-shaping and polishing processes. There are other bright metal auto trim parts you will need to restore using different industrial processes, including machine straightening, welding, and plating.

Die-cast metal—"pot metal"—was used to make auto trim for some 50–60 years. Pot metal parts were easy and cheap to make, but deteriorated quickly. For years, pot metal was considered unrepairable. When the author got involved in car collecting in the mid-1970s, the focus was on replacing pot metal, rather than fixing it. Today, restorers have pot metal repair services at their disposal.

Bumpers are an important type of trim that restorers have to deal with. They are made of heavy, common steel that is chrome or nickel plated. Fixing a bumper is rarely a home restoration job. There are companies that specialize only in restoring bumpers and bumper parts.

A half-restored '39 Chrysler nose displayed by the Chrome Co. illustrates the difference between a "barn find" and a car that's been well restored. Note how nicely the restored bright trim sets off the work. *Jesse Gunnell*

Bumpers are an important type of trim restorers fix. They're made of plated common steel. Fixing a heavy bumper isn't a home restoration job. Some firms specialize in restoring bumpers and bumper parts.

Trim insert panels are another item that can be a bear to restore properly. Especially on 1950s cars—and a few 1950s trucks—such panels came in different colors and textures, with finishes ranging from anodized to wood-grained.

Since plating plays a large part in restoring metal trim parts on a collector car that aren't stainless steel, aluminum, brass, or copper, let's take a look at how plating is done. Then, we'll discuss pot metal restoration. Finally, we'll look at a few of the specific parts we'll deal with like front end trim, bumpers, and insert panels.

CHROME PLATING

Almost all plating processes are based on an electrolytic process. The parts being plated are placed in a tank filled with liquid (electrolyte) that conducts electricity, making a DC circuit. A bar of plating material is the anode (+) and the piece to be plated is the cathode (-). When the circuit is switched on, current travels from anode to cathode and carries tiny pieces of the plating material to the part. The plater changes the plating material, electrolyte, and amperage to plate different metals.

Although chromium is a costly metal, very little is used. The true expense in plating is in preparation of the piece. Two similar pieces could vary in plating cost if one has more pitting.

In normal chroming, the pits are removed by the polishing operations before copper plating. If the pits are too deep, the polishing will turn the pits into holes that go all the way through the metal. When pot metal repairs are done, each pit is filled with solder or special epoxy. Pits cannot be filled with plating material.

If a customer has many identical parts in similar shape, they can be done faster and the cost drops. The plater will study the condition and complexity of each piece and set a price. If he gets the go-ahead, he may engrave the owner's name on the back and photograph the piece. It is then stripped to its base metal. Muriatic acid is used to strip stamped steel, forgings, or fabricated pieces. Die cast is stripped electrically in a sulfuric acid bath.

Steel, zinc alloy, or aluminum parts are polished, copper struck, and plated, polished, nickel-plated, and finally chrome-plated. With copper or nickel, the initial polishing and copper striking/plating aren't required and nickel doesn't need to be nickel-plated. Brass parts go through all steps except copper plating.

Some shops advertise triple chrome plating. That doesn't mean three layers of chrome. Terry Meetz of Custom Plating Services says parts get plated three times, starting with copper, which is soft enough to fill tiny imperfections and polishes to a high sheen. The level of brilliance the copper is brought to determines the chrome's final appearance.

The next metal plated on is nickel, which adds a silvery color and protects the copper from corrosion. In the early days of automaking, the process stopped here. However, nickel oxidizes slowly, taking on a yellow tint. That is why a very thin coat of chrome is added. It resists oxidation and adds a nice bluish tint.

Custom Plating Services specializes in show chrome and gives parts two "baths" in copper tanks. After some initial prep with a sander on grinder mode with 150-grit paper, the part is racked and put into the copper tank for $1\frac{1}{2}$ hours. The copper is then sanded with 320- and 800-grit papers. Then, the part goes in for a 1-hour coat of copper. This second coat is buffed out.

The part is reracked, cleaned, and readied for nickel plating. It goes into the nickel tank for about 20 minutes, getting a nice silvery layer. It is cleaned again, before spending a mere 20–30 seconds in a chrome tank. This thin sealing coat may go on fast, but it gives the part its long-lasting, bright, blue-tinted shine.

The insert panels frequently used on mid-1950s cars is another special type of trim you may need to restore. Some are painted, some are anodized or plated, and some have unique textures.

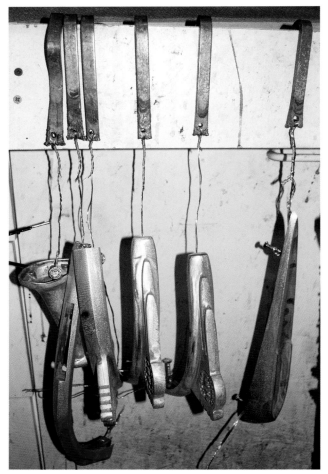

Between trips to the copper, nickel, or chrome-plating tanks, the parts are hung up like this to air dry.

POT METAL PARTS

Pot metal is the nickname for alloys that automakers used to quickly and cheaply manufacture castings for hood mascots, door handles, headlight doors, trunk handles, and other parts. Pot metal parts have inconsistent makeups, but are always made of zinc combined with a bunch of metals including lead, copper, tin, iron, magnesium, aluminum, and more.

Pot metals melt at low temperatures, which production planners liked because this made parts easy to form. However, it wasn't called "monkey metal" for nothing. Restorers have found repairing pot metal to be a problem. If you try to weld it using normal welding techniques, it will melt.

Pot metal ages quickly. It is made of fast-oxidizing "active" metals. You have probably seen pot metal auto parts or car toys that are bent, warped, twisted, cracked, and blistered. Zinc's low boiling point and the fast cooling of the pot metal parts promotes the retention of air bubbles in the castings, making them porous and prone to rapid corrosion. Pot metal is also hard to replate, because it suffers surface corrosion that blisters and flakes the chrome, as well as internal corrosion due to its porosity.

Repairing Pot Metal

Pot metal was once impossible to repair. Today, we have solders and glues like J. B. Weld, Muggy Weld rods, and Caswell Electroplating's Solder-It Pot Metal Repair (see Appendix) that home restorers can use to repair pot metal. Some work as out-of-a-tube fillers and others are low-melting-point solders. Muggy Weld's 350-degree rod is made of "Super Alloy 1" and bonds at about half the melting point of pot metal. A flux changes colors when the base metal hits the

After the copper dries, a Custom Plating Specialists technician, or Terry himself, will carefully inspect the copper plating.

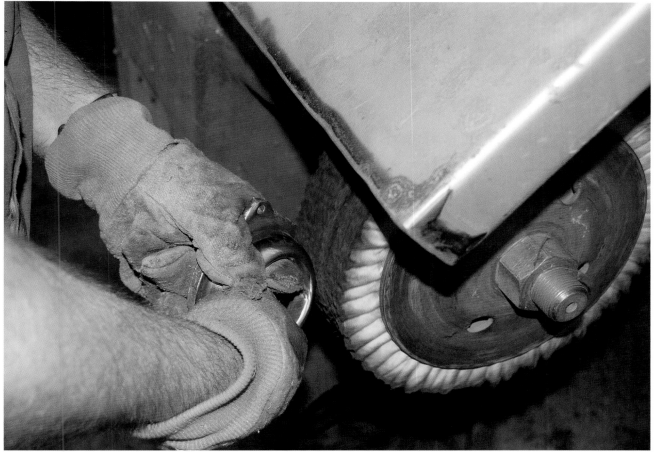
The copper base coat has to be buffed smooth. Nickel or chrome plating would highlight any imperfections left in the piece.

right temperature. These products work well for painted parts and toys, and sellers claim they can be plated over.

Since most classic car parts require plating, a better option is a company that offers pot metal repairs. Most plating companies in the Appendix can do this and some specialize. They start by stripping all of the old plating off the part and sandblasting it. They then drill out the pits like a dentist does and give them "fillings" made of selected metals. The filling and metalwork has to be done carefully, so the part retains its original form and detail as much as possible. The filled parts are hand-sanded smooth, prior to replating.

Refinishing or Replating

Each pot metal repair service available to old-car hobbyists does things slightly differently, but the basic process begins with the smoothed and repaired part taking a lengthy bath in the copper plating tank. After four to six hours or so, it is removed and a series of hand-sanding and polishing operations begins.

The polishing continues until the part looks like gleaming copper. Then, it is cleaned up in an acid bath,

before getting a shorter bath in the nickel tank and a quick dip in the chrome tank. It is cleaned before each immersion. After final polishing operations, the part is ready for reinstallation, hopefully on an equally gleaming collector car.

"There are limits on what we can do to repair and refinish a broken piece of pot metal," Meetz told us. "Each pot metal casting has a different makeup and composition, because that's the nature of the beast with zinc die-cast castings."

Each casting has also undergone different types of deterioration with a range of results. Pot metal repair is like doing a puzzle, but luckily for modern restorers, "monkey metal" can be tamed.

SPECIAL FRONT END CONSIDERATIONS: MASCOTS, GRILLES, AND ORNAMENTS

Front-end trim is subjected to more wear. It gets "sandblasted" by debris from passing cars. Hood mascots (like the Packard "pelican") are usually pot metal. Most grilles are made of harder metal. Hood ornaments (like shield-shaped Ford crests) are pot metal or stainless.

This engine trim, a valve cover, is at the drying stage after a bath in the nickel-plating tank. Bumpers and larger parts are plated using a similar system, but in larger tanks, of course.

Pot metal mascots develop "pimples" and flaky chrome plating. Before ordering expensive repairs, check if reproductions are available. Many one-make catalogs offer reproductions. Don Sommer's American Arrow Corp. makes them for classic cars. An NOS mascot is a rare alternative that will fetch a handsome price.

Most classics had steel grilles. If your grille was nickel-plated, a chrome-plated grille won't look right. Some reproductions are available. You may find NOS grille pieces. Factory grilles made during the Korean War may have thin plating covered by lacquer (done to preserve chromium). The thin chrome doesn't hold up. If you find such parts, have them replated with regular chrome before installing them. Around 1959, Detroit began using aluminum grilles. Aluminum was used because it was rust resistant, not for weight savings. Aluminum grilles can be restored and buffed.

With all restored front end parts, an important factor is retaining the original detail and crispness of line. A good metalworker and plater will be able to restore a piece without losing too much of its original design detail.

Bumpers

Model A Ford bumpers were straight, flat, and hard to dent or bend. By the time the 1950s arrived, bumpers had curves, Dagmars, lights set into them, and indentations for styling or housing license plates. You might be able to repair a Model A bumper with a 20-ton press from Harbor Freight and some polishing supplies. Straightening and chroming a 1959 Caddy bumper would require more talent and tools.

The basic steps in bumper restoration include repair of pits, rust holes, and collision damage like dents and twists. The bumper has to be returned to original shape (straight or otherwise) if deformed. The old chrome and other substrates have to be stripped off before the bumper can be replated with copper, nickel, and chrome. In addition to the bumper itself, you may have to have bumper guards and end wings restored.

Replace or Repair?

Before absorbing the expense of a restored bumper, you might want to look into buying either an NOS replacement or a reproduction. These are available for some popular cars from catalog houses. You can also find them on eBay, but be careful. We purchased new bumpers for an MG TF on eBay. When they arrived, the holes did not match up with the bumper brackets. They were either defective reproductions or kit car bumpers. They looked new, but didn't fit.

Some companies regularly buy and restore collector car bumpers and resell them on an exchange basis. Before sending your originals in as a core, make sure you're getting an *exact* replacement. There are horror stories on the Internet about honest mistakes. With high shipping costs, the safest way to deal with such suppliers is face to face at swap meets.

Straightening and Grinding the Bumper

Minor impacts will leave small dents in a bumper and these will be hammered out by hand from the rear. As the dents disappear, the metal will straighten and go back to its original shape. The process is just like straightening trim, but larger hammers are used. Some restorers may use a hammer and dolly or a large spoon. For larger dents, a hydraulic press will have to be used.

Grinding comes next. The restorer will use a grinder to remove large pits and imperfections in the bumper metal. Brass will be used to weld up holes in the bumper bar and if the holes are due to corrosion, all of the rust will have to be chemically removed or ground back until the restorer gets to good, solid, rust-free metal. Cracks in the metal can also be fixed with brass.

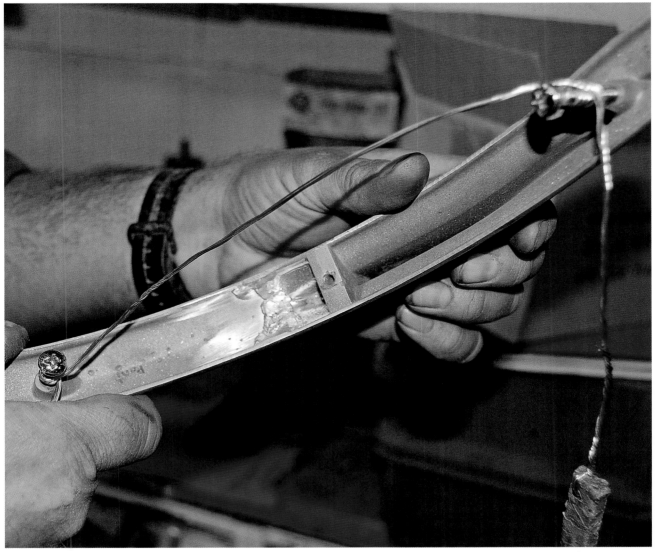

Note how the copper electrodes have been attached to this vintage tractor ornament. In the tank, the copper will migrate from the electrode to the pot metal trim.

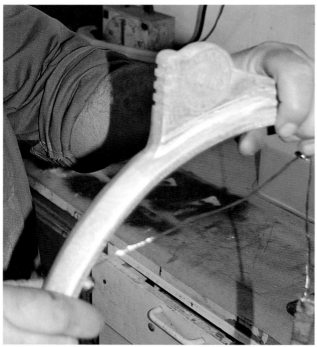

Here we see Terry Meetz holding the same piece of trim for an old tractor at a different stage in the plating process. Plating bright metal can't be rushed.

Polishing the Bumper

After repairs are made, the metal has to be polished using different-grit polishing wheels. As it is smoothed and the imperfections are disappearing, the metal will take on a mirror finish. An experienced restorer will accomplish this without creating warping or distortion. When the bumper is plated in the first phase of the chroming process, soft copper will fill any minor imperfections.

Some restorers offer to polish the back of the bumper to a mirror finish as an option. Terry Meetz, at Custom Plating Service, suggests that customers may want to paint the back of a bumper with silver Rustoleum. Bumpers that jut pretty far out from the car body are seen on some prewar cars. The backs of the bumper bars show and always look much better if painted.

Replating

The bumper is plated the same as other parts, with an initial coat of copper to seal the metal and provide good adhesion. Next comes a soft copper "primer" coat that builds up the surface prior to polishing. When the copper looks mirrorlike, it's time to apply nickel plating. After more polishing, if any problems are found, the polishing and plating continue until the bumper looks perfect. Then, it's ready for a very thin coat of chrome.

Restorer Jerry Kopecky, of Kopecky Klassics in Iola, Wisconsin, focuses on restoring finned Chrysler cars. As you can see, his specialty requires him to order lot of chrome-plating work.

Custom Plating Specialists will have to disassemble this '41 Chevy truck grille before they can replate the individual parts.

The back side is generally blasted clean and plated with copper and nickel. Chrome plates the back of some but not all bumpers. Like paint, chrome adheres well in some spots and poorly in others. It may just run off the rear contour of many bumpers. Since it's unpolished, the back of the bumper will also be rougher than the front. It's advisable to paint the back side to reduce the chance of rust.

Insert Panels

The most famous trim insert is the white anodized "house siding" used on the '57 Chevy Bel Air. The gold-textured trim used on some '57 Fords runs a close second. However, the use of such panels did not originate on postwar cars. Some high-dollar prewar classics had contrasting-color inserts between their belt moldings to give added eye appeal. When such cars are restored, it can require great ingenuity and creativity to replicate the color, pattern, and texture of inserts.

In the case of the '57 Chevy, reproduction trim is available, but that is the exception, not the rule. If you're restoring many other cars, coming up with side trim inserts to replace damaged originals on your project car can be a big problem. Most likely, you'll first try salvage yards across the country to find decent originals to restore. Failing in that, several repair options are possible.

Repairing Trim Inserts

Most inserts are made of sheet metal that can be restored like other trim. They can be hammered, sanded, polished, and even buffed to straighten and refinish the metal. If you are restoring

an original panel, textures the automaker used will already be in the sheet metal. If you're fabricating a replacement from scratch, you'll have to find ways to reproduce the textures. Some simple ones can be replicated by hand, but you may have to look around for a metal fabrication company that can press or roll textures into metal. If it was done in making the car, it can somehow be duplicated today.

If there are breaks or tears in the panel that have to be repaired, it can be special-soldered, brazed, or welded. Sheet metal is thin, so you'll have to use proper welding techniques. Suppliers like Eastwood and others listed in the Appendix have tech reps that can suggest specific repair methods to suit your particular situation.

Refinishing

Special plating processes such as copper plating, *satin chrome* (plated over coarse copper); *matte chrome* (plated over copper treated with a vapor hone of water and glass beads); *Butler finish* (done by using a slurry of pumice and water on the copper); and *black chrome* (using a special catalyst with the chrome layer) provide a variety of finishes.

At this year's Bloomington Gold swap meet, M+M Custom Finishing of Bristol, Illinois, demonstrated a water transfer printing system by which objects can be three-dimensionally decorated using the principle of water pressure application. It makes it possible to print an endless array of patterns—and textures—on flat or contoured objects without leaving voids or seams. This process—fully described in M+M's brochures—seems well suited for refinishing trim inserts.

Chapter 8
Specially Finished Metal Trim and Genuine Wood Trim

While buffed or plated metal serves nicely as auto trim, other sections of a car may have metal parts that were specially finished for eye appeal. We could never forget the beautiful woodgrained window trim on the '49 De Soto that our father purchased when we were kids. The De Soto was a midpriced car, but the woodgrained metal made us feel as if we were riding in a Duesenberg.

Wood trim works particularly well on car interiors and the exterior of certain models (like the Chrysler Town & Country or Ford Country Squire). Most early cars had genuine wood trim, and it can still be found inside certain models. Simulated woodgrain trim is another possibility that appeared by the mid-1930s, if not earlier. Simulated woodgrain trim is usually manufactured through a veneering process, although water transfer printing is another option today.

In addition to wood grains, cars have been produced with simulated canework, plaid, floral, and paisley finishes and even psychedelic patterns on the roof (in the "psycho '70s"). The restorer who wants to put cars back to original condition has to come up with ways to restore such unusual trims.

Painted bright metal trim and *cloisonné* may also require restoration. Luckily, over the 75-80 years that hobbyists have been restoring old cars, various industrial processes have been developed for such jobs.

Simulated woodgrain trim can be found on the dashboards and door panels of cars from the 1930s up and on such things as consoles in later cars. Restoration methods can vary according to vehicle age.

Real wood trim was common on prewar cars and can also be found on postwar models like the Chrysler Town & Country and MG Magnette. Real wood trim is making a comeback on cars today.

Classic car hubcaps and wheel covers were often trimmed with red, black, or white paint and sometimes with more than one color. Some had only colored writing and some had elaborate painted grid or fin designs.

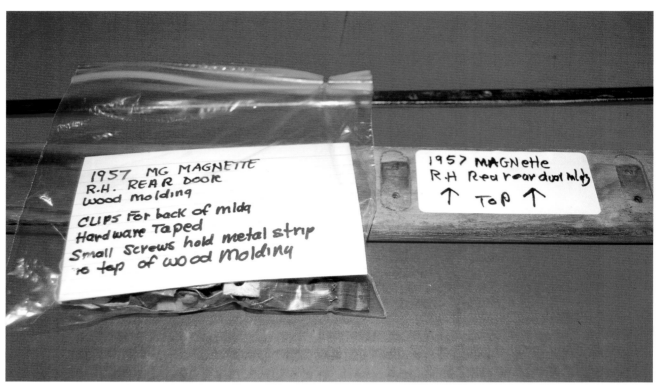

Put small parts in a baggie. Put a labeled index card inside. The baggie has been attached to the metal molding with an electrical tie. Later, the molding will be buffed. Also, mark the "top" of the wood molding.

After stripping old varnish off the wood, sand with 80-grit paper on a jitterbug sander. If you are sanding ash (not the case here), use a natural-colored filler with minimum shrinkage to smooth the surface.

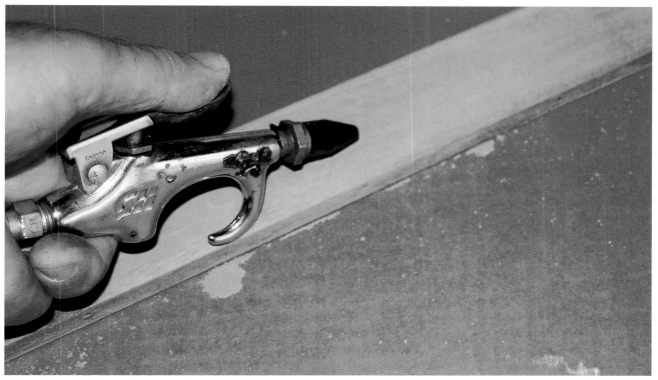

Having a clean work environment is important. After your initial sanding, blow any fine wood dust off the part with a compressed air gun or nozzle.

REPAIRING GENUINE WOOD TRIM

Two types of real wood are used commonly in automobiles: ash and maple. These are long-lasting hardwoods with a natural resistance to wood-boring insects. Hardwoods are dense, which makes them fire resistant. Another plus is they can hold fasteners more securely. This keeps screws from working loose. Ash and maple are used primarily for structural components, which restorers may have to refinish. Among the Big Three, GM and Chrysler favored ash and Ford favored maple. Birch and dark ribbon-grained mahogany are other woods used for nonstructural trim pieces.

The restorer must determine the type of wood a damaged part is made of and decide whether the piece can be repaired and refinished. In many cases, it may be better to make a new piece. To make these decisions, some disassembly of the car or trim may be required.

The first step is to treat the wood with a stripper that will lift the old finish and allow you to restore the dirty, blackened grain. Follow can directions. The stripper will probably leave some stubborn spots that need to be sanded.

Hand-sand with 80-grit paper on a jitterbug sander. After initial sanding, blow fine wood dust off the part with compressed air. If you are sanding ash, the harder layers that make the grain will stand up. You will have to use a natural-colored filler with minimum shrinkage to smooth the surface.

Treat the wood with a clear lacquer sanding sealer, and then use a high-quality spar varnish to refinish it. You want the varnish to bring out a yellow tint and highlight the darker grain.

Put the filler on across the grain and let it set up until its glossiness is gone. Then wipe it off, again moving against the grain. Most fillers require a full day to cure, and the longer the better. Fully cured filler will sand better. Sand the fully cured filler using fine sandpaper on a sanding block, checking smoothness with your hand.

With any wood, when you get to smooth, bare wood, blow off the sanding dust. Treat the wood with a clear lacquer sanding sealer, and then use a high-quality spar varnish to refinish it. You want the varnish to bring out a yellow tint and highlight the darker grain. Apply a two-part epoxy coating to protect the finish.

If it's necessary to replace damaged parts, your own level of woodworking skill comes into play. If you have done woodworking, you'll have a good idea of your abilities. First timers may want to enroll in an adult education class that teaches woodworking or buy books or CDs on the topic. In other cases, you may want to send the part to a professional shop like one of those listed in the Appendix.

WOOD VENEERING

Wood veneering is a process used to make woodgrained auto parts. Dennis Bickford of Vintage Woodworks in Iola, Wisconsin, is an expert in this craft. Dennis reproduces the veneered inserts for Chrysler Town & Countrys. This same 10-hour process is used to make woodgrained interior trim parts like dashboard panels, garnish moldings, center console inserts, steering wheel inserts and so on.

According to Dennis, 12 inserts—made of wood pressed onto metal panels—are needed to restore a Chrysler Town & Country. Six are flat panels and six have compound curves. Bickford has been making panels for a long time and has accurate patterns for each one. He starts by having sheet metal panels cut to fit his patterns. The panels with compound curves are shaped with an English wheel (One hard-to-reproduce panel is available in fiberglass).

The holes in the steel Chrysler Town & Country panel are for mounting the brake lamp and associated wiring.

This steel panel for a Chrysler Town & Country will have the wood veneer panel glued to it. Dennis Bickford, of Vintage Woodworks in Iola, Wisconsin, reproduces these panels, because they are often missing.

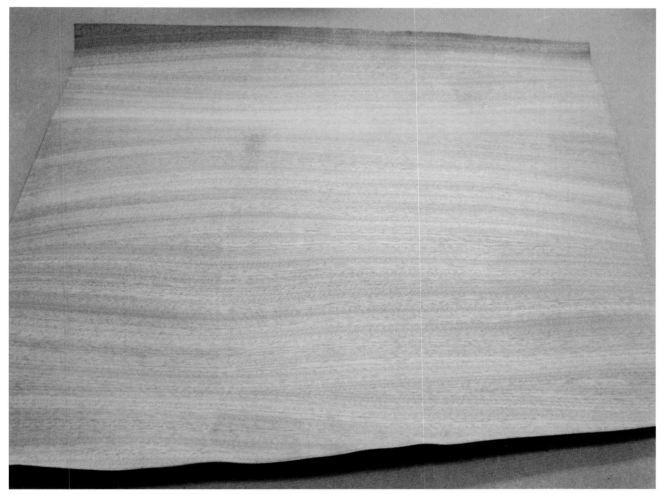

Bickford first puts his precut veneer on top of the steel panel in a 1-ton vacuum press. This starts to make the wood veneer conform to the steel panel, as in this postpress photo. Both are marked so they can be indexed when glued together later on.

Restoration processes are often different from factory production methods. Chrysler made the panels by gluing wood veneer to flat panels and shaping them in a stamping machine. Dennis says this process led to premature panel failures. Instead of repeating Chrysler's mistake, Bickford cuts the veneer slightly larger than his metal panel, and then places the panel and veneer into a vacuum press where it stays for 24 hours. The vacuum press applies 2,000 psi to form the veneer to the contours of the metal panel. The vacuum press slowly shapes the wood veneer so that it "learns" the form it will need to take from the metal panel. No gluing is done at this stage. Dennis gets a perfectly shaped wood veneer that fits the panel like a glove, with no wrinkles. Both pieces are marked for realignment.

Before gluing, the metal panel must be prepped. Sometimes the original metal panel is reused, but often a new one is needed. Regardless, the metal has to be sanded with a 36-grit disc. On reused panels, this removes all of the old veneer. On both, it roughs up the metal's surface to help the glue adhere better.

After the panel has the correct roughness, Dennis washes it three times with acetone to remove grease, sanding dust, and dirt. When it is cleaned and dried, a two-part marine epoxy is mixed up and applied to the metal panel using a one-time-use sponge roller that produces a more even coat than a brush. Next, the shaped wood veneer panel is sandwiched with the metal panel, while lining up the alignment marks made earlier. Since the wood veneer is larger than the metal panel, it has to be shaved to the correct size.

Dennis tapes the two panels together at top and bottom, puts them back in the vacuum press, applies pressure, and allows the epoxy to cure for 24 hours. When the sandwich comes out of the press, it will be spotted with epoxy that flowed through pores in the wood. A light brushing with a cabinet scraper removes the white spots.

A powder type aniline dye is applied to refinish the surface of the wood veneer. Bickford finds that this gives a clearer view of the wood and grain than an oil-based stain.

The metal panels (original or reproduction) are sanded with 36-grit disks. This removes all traces of the factory veneer and also roughs up the smooth metal for better glue adhesion.

A West System epoxy is applied to enhance bonding. When it dries, several coats of varnish or urethane are applied. The veneer is sanded between each coat so the finish gets smoother and smoother. When finished, the wood veneer panel will have a shiny luster to it.

RESTORING NONWOODGRAINED FINISHES

What if you were restoring an early postwar Willys station wagon with canework trim or if you were building a Resto-Mod and wanted to replicate a carbon fiber texture on the side trim insert? You can do this using a water transfer printing (WTP) process now being promoted by M+M Custom Finishes of Bristol, Illinois.

We described the WTP process earlier in this book, but it bears repeating here. It can be used to transfer an endless number of patterns on flat or compound curved surfaces without voids or seams. The process is done in four stages as follows:

Stage 1
A. Surface of items to be decorated is sanded to accept primer.
B. Primer is applied.
C. Base coat is applied.
D. Drying is carried out.

Stage 2
A. Film is cut to match size and shape of item being decorated.
B. Chemical activator applied to film.

Stage 3
A. Item slowly immersed in tank.
B. Item is removed from tank after complete submersion.

Stage 4
A. Item is immediately washed and dried.
B. High- or low-sheen acrylic finish is applied.

A liberal amount of acetone is poured on top of the steel Chrysler Town & Country panel to totally eliminate contaminants that might keep the epoxy—or glue—from adhering.

Dennis Bickford always uses a scale to get the proper mixture of West System 105 Epoxy Resin and West System 207 Hardener. He follows the directions on the can to determine the proportions.

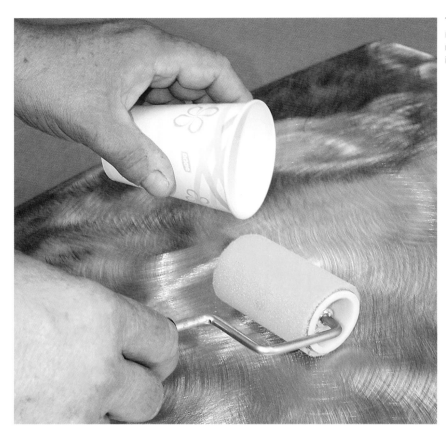

To evenly apply the two-part epoxy to all areas of the metal panel, Vintage Woodworks uses a small, disposable roller like this one designed for painting corners. The roller is used only once.

Applying the veneer to the epoxied metal panel is the next step. Bickford matches up the index marks he made earlier for an exact fit. He then tapes the indexed pieces together and puts them through a press.

REPAIRING SIMULATED WOODGRAIN

In some restorations, it may not be necessary to replace wood veneer parts. For example, you may own a muscle car with a wood-trimmed center console that looks faded and cracked around the gear shift lever. Often, the cracks will appear to be in the finish, rather than in the wood veneer.

Unfortunately, cracks in the clear topcoat usually go into the veneer, because the clear also cracks where it soaked into the veneer when originally applied. To get rid of such cracks, you must sand slightly into the veneer. Usually, this will force you to sand the entire panel into the veneer to make the color uniform. If you're very lucky, you'll be able to paint the color back into that panel using acrylic artists' paints or stain pens. However, this rarely works.

When sanding, keep in mind that some automotive interior veneers are very thin. Sand very lightly and use very fine-grit papers. On more modern cars, the veneer is applied to plastic and it's easy to go through to the plastic panel.

Most likely, the sanded area will come out a different shade. It will be in the same color family, but noticeably different from the rest of the trim in the car's interior. To make things match again, you will need to sand all of the wood trim. After all of the wood trim is sanded, you will have to refinish every piece with the same clear epoxy. This will make the interior look like new again, but the job of doing the entire interior can take as long as three months to complete.

The best clear epoxies for this job are available at automotive paint shops. Stay away from epoxies sold by home improvement stores. The better the quality of the epoxy, the better the interior will look and the longer it will last. Most high-end modern cars use nitro cellulous lacquer for the clear coat. Polyurethane varnish will look similar. A two-part catalyzed urethane clear is acceptable, and it should be applied with a spray gun for best results.

Clear that comes out of rattle cans takes a long time to dry and usually doesn't hold up well. However, companies

The wood veneer panel and the metal Chrysler Town & Country panel are glued together and sandwiched in a 2000-pound press. Since the veneer was cut a little larger, it has to be trimmed to the shape of the metal panel.

After several coats of wood stain, each followed by hand-sanding, the panel arrives at its finished state, and looks like a piece of fine furniture. It is glossy enough to reflect the lights in Dennis Bickford's Vintage Woodworks shop.

like Eastwood (see Appendix) have special rattle can formulas and sprayers created for hobbyists. They are more expensive than what you'll find in discount department stores, but they are worth the extra money in the long run.

We talked above about the new water transfer printing process that M+M Custom Finishing was promoting at the Bloomington Gold swap meet. Among other things, it can be used to apply custom woodgrain finishes to plastic or metal parts. Burl and walnut finishes are specifically mentioned in the company's brochure, but the company says "any" wood finish can be duplicated.

CLOISONNÉ

Cloisonné trim is usually made of copper, silver, or gold decorated with powdered glass that is fired in an oven until the glass becomes red hot and melts to a smooth finish over the metal or part of the metal.

Cloisonné trim is among the most beautiful bright metal trim you will see on restored vintage cars. It was originally

created by enameling the metal parts. Enamels are complex combinations of clear glass, color-adding metal oxides, and other materials that are melted together.

Emblemagic of Grand River, Ohio, one of the leading restorers of cloisonné trim, separates the trim into three categories: Pre-1930, 1930–1939, 1940 and up. The prettiest cloisonné trim is like "jewelry for cars."

Restoration of cloisonné car badges and enamel emblems includes minor metal repair or straightening, repairing attachment studs, replacing the enamel, and replating the metal. All of the original vitreous enamel that has deteriorated must be removed before the metal can be repaired. In most cases, repairs made to the metal are similar to those described for pot metal.

After damage to the metal has been taken care of, new vitreous enamel is applied and fired onto the emblem (AKA *champlevé* or *cloisonné* emblem). Modern restorers may also use synthetic resins, composites, cold enamels, cold-cast bronzes, and polymer clays to get certain colors or effects.

Emblemagic was wise enough to stockpile obsolete, lead-bearing enamels like the original types, which can no longer be legally manufactured. The company uses only these enamels in its restorations. This is a big help in matching some old, hard-to-reproduce original colors.

According to the Emblemagic website (see Appendix), an emblem restoration will usually run about 12 to 16 weeks. The company groups the emblems into batches, which are done only a couple of times a year. The website states that cost is determined by the size, number of colors, type of colors, and complexity of the design, as well as any metal or stud repair that may be required. The average, simple, medium-sized emblem with one or two colors—like a Ford emblem—will run about $260. Emblems that have translucent colors, with everything else remaining equal, will run about $295.

Before spending "big bucks" to have the cloisonné trim on your collector car restored, check to see if reproductions are available. Mail order parts houses may have the piece you need or a one-marque club may have reproduced it as a club project. Home restorers seeking to save money may use also replating and painting (below) to restore cloisonné emblems and get fairly good results. However, there is nothing like the real thing if you're after a 100-point restoration.

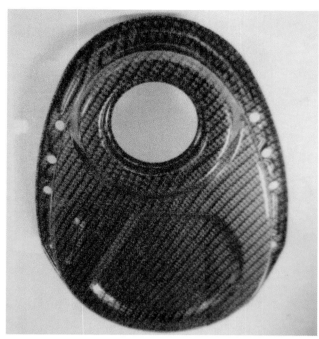

M+M Custom Finishes can transfer an endless number of patterns onto flat or compound curved surfaces without voids or seams. The process, which is done in four stages, produced this customized engine timing cover.

Simulated woodgrain finishes, as on this '36 Pontiac dash, can be reproduced using various stains over a base coat. Dennis Bickford of Vintage Woodworks uses varied methods to make different grains.

The simulated woodgrain on this '70 Dodge Challenger at Nickey Chicago is actually a plastic veneer. It can be reproduced by hand through an "antiquing" process or by water transfer printing.

NAMEPLATES, EMBLEMS, AND BADGES

The chrome-plated metal nameplates that spell out the name or model of a car in block letters or script are prone to two types of breakage that can be repaired with relative ease. Often the studs on the back of the trim piece that pass through holes in the car body will break off. About 20 percent of the time, the trim piece itself will be fractured or will break during removal from the car.

A broken stud must be carefully drilled out. You can then fashion a replacement out of a small, fine-thread bolt. Use an two-part epoxy to hold the new stud in place.

A fractured nameplate can be fixed by using brass rod to join two pieces back together. Many nameplates are produced in a way that leaves a groove on the back of them. If your nameplate has a flat back, you can cut a groove in it with a small grinder or Dremel tool. Then, buy a small-diameter piece of brass rod and cut off about an inch of it. Fit it into the groove. If the nameplate letters have curves,

you'll need to bend the rod. When the trim pieces and the rod all fit together well, use your epoxy to bond everything together. Sand the back until flat. If the crack shows, have the piece replated.

Many emblems have an indented area that is enameled or painted in a color. Red and black are most common, but white, blue, yellow, and other colors are also used. To have a trim piece properly enameled, you may want to send it out to a specialist like Emblemagic. But you can handle painted trim yourself.

If the emblem needs to be repaired or replated, take care of that first. Then, wearing protective gear, use acetone to remove the old finish. After toweling and air drying the piece, spray the entire piece with the proper color enamel and allow it to dry for 24 hours. Then use enamel reducer to remove the paint from the raised areas. If you are careful not to get reducer in the indented area, only the color you sprayed will remain there and the trim will look like new.

Chapter 9
"Chrome-Plated" Plastic Trim

OVERVIEW OF RESTORING CHROME PLASTIC TRIM

The shiny, silvery plastic parts you see on the interior of your late postwar collector car are not really "chromed" (chrome-plated). They are actually made by a vacuum metalizing process in which aluminum is vaporized in a vacuum chamber and applied to the plastic parts. If expertly done, the resulting chromelike finish will stand up pretty well to driver and passenger use. However, it does not have the durability and corrosive resistance of real chrome plating and will not weather well. That's why you won't find vacuum metalized parts being used on the outside of your car.

Your car may have a chrome plastic grille, but it was not made through the vacuum metalized process. Most likely, it was "chromed" using a very special electroplating process that can put "real" chrome on certain types of plastics. The major automakers have these parts made by large companies with specialized equipment. The process is also expensive. The automakers use such parts because they save weight over metal, not because they are cheaper to make than metal parts. The electroplated plastic parts are made by the tens of thousands, in China or other foreign countries, and the high volume of parts made helps bring the cost into a reasonable range.

In the old days, trim like this 1940s Buick grille used to be made of metal. They were sturdy, but heavy and prone to rust.

This '50 Buick trunk handle has an insert made of a crystal clear plastic with colors applied to the back. Repairs can be made by removing remaining old paint and using candy apple paint or nail polish to recolor. *Jesse Gunnell*

It is virtually impossible and very impractical for the hobbyist to carry out either of these "plating" processes in a home restoration shop. However, a relatively large number of companies currently offer vacuum metalizing services to hobbyists. In addition, Paul's Chrome Plating, of Evans City, Pennsylvania, is now promoting a service in which it encases a plastic part in copper and then electroplates the part. Hobbyists can deal with these firms by mail order.

Anytime you decide to send a rare and valuable vintage car part to an outside restoration services company, it pays to check the company's reputation. You may be able to find another member of your local or national car club who has dealt with the company. The company may sell its services on eBay or another auction website and have a public feedback history. It also pays to put the company's name into a search engine and see what comes up about it on discussion boards. If you do not use a computer, you can check with the Better

Business Bureau in the company's hometown to see if it has drawn complaints.

Wise customers will also call or email a company to discuss things like safe shipping practices (both ways), the tagging and tracking of parts, insurance practices, turnaround times on their work, customer service, and warranties. Some hobby companies are small, one-person operations that do a great job.

For the hobbyist on a limited budget who can't afford outside professional services, Eastwood offers two types of paints that can be brushed or sprayed on plastic parts to restore a close-to-original appearance. The first is called Liquid Chrome, and the second is marketed as Almost Chrome. Other suppliers probably sell similar products, but we have never had much luck with store-bought chrome paints. These Eastwood paints do work well when properly applied. They are certainly the cheapest way to get the parts restored, if you have the skill to use them expertly.

Jerry Kopecky restored these emblems for a 1960 Chrysler 300 F by painting the colors from the back. The right modern paints should last longer than the finishes used in the 1950s and 1960s. *Jesse Gunnell*

As cars got newer, plastic-chrome parts were used more and more. This '89 Caprice 9C1 police car has "chromed" plastic parts all across the rear end. They don't rust, but if they break, repair can be a problem.

HISTORY

Bakelite was probably the first plastic used in the manufacture of auto parts. Bakelite is based on the thermosetting phenol formaldehyde resin *polyoxybenzylmethylenglycolanhydride*, which was developed in Belgium in the 1907–1909 era. It is made through the reaction of phenol and formaldehyde under heat and pressure. A wood flour filler is usually used in the manufacturing process, and you will see different-color brown specks if you try polishing bakelite.

Bakelite was the first plastic made from synthetic components. It does not conduct heat or electricity and was also used to make dash knobs (especially cigar lighter knobs) and some electrical component housings. Bakelite is glossy when new, but usually dulls with age. Polishing will make it shine, but also brings out the unattractive brown specks.

Although this chapter is not about Bakelite, it is interesting to note that its original shiny appearance can be restored by using a product called Pensbury Manor Black Hard Rubber Pen Potion No. 9–Black Hard Rubber Dye, which was originally used in the restoration of vintage fountain pens. This product was actually developed by Syd Saperstein, a T-Series MG collector (email wahlnut@pensburymanor.com).

By the mid-1930s, most cars had white or black plastic dashboard knobs and other plastic interior parts. In general, the use of plastic in industry was growing and the auto industry was a logical target for plastic sales. In 1939, Rohm and Hass, of Philadelphia, helped General Motors create a Pontiac sedan with clear Plexiglas body panels for exhibit at the New York World's Fair and the Golden Gate Exposition in San Francisco. Two of these cars, both different, were eventually built, and one survives today in the collection of Frank Kleptz of Terre Haute, Indiana.

By the 1950s, the use of plastic had grown even more and some cars even had exterior plastic parts. The shield-shaped Ford badge is a good example. It had both colors and a metalized gold stripe. Pontiacs of this era had a red circular

In addition to a chromelike look, plastic trim can be refinished with other "bright metal" appearances, such as the satin silver used on these '89 Caprice door moldings.

Aluminum finishes are very popular on plastic wheels, like these five-spoke aftermarket wheels seen on a '94 Pontiac Sunbird convertible. Real aluminum wheels would tarnish quickly, but these won't.

The bright-metal finish around the A/C vent looks fine, but note the dark (black) section on the horizontal strip below the vent. Interestingly, this same spot was bad on both sides of this '89 Caprice dash.

A thin paintbrush (see inset photo) with a dab of Eastwood's Almost Chrome paint on it can be used to refinish the gap in the plastic chrome stripe and detail this '89 Caprice dash.

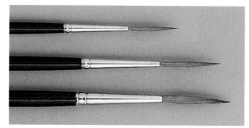

Eastwood sells these small detailing brushes. *Eastwood*

grille badge with a metalized Pontiac Indian head logo that had a circular, metalized stripe around it. These elements were chrome colored, except in 1951. That was Pontiac's 25th anniversary year, and the Indian head and circular stripe were metalized gold.

These plastic emblems and inserts were actually made of a crystal clear plastic with colors applied to the back. Then, a light grayish coating was put over the baked-on colors. A reasonable repair of a damaged plastic trim piece of this type can be made by removing remnants of the old colors and using enamel paint or nail polish (on the red Pontiac inserts) to recolor the back of the piece.

The early 1950s also saw the first use of plastics (fiberglass) in the manufacture of automobile bodies. The Kaiser-Darrin was the first fiberglass-bodied production car, but the Corvette was close behind.

In the 1960s, the use of chrome-plated plastic parts began. Such components as dashboard bezels, interior door moldings, and armrest bases with chromelike platings were seen. A vacuum metalizing process was used to produce these parts. They were not very durable and the chromelike coating often peeled off like tin foil, leaving bare off-white plastic showing. The "chrome plastic" parts did look good when new and were used into the 1970s, at least.

REPLACING

The term "replacing"—as applied to plastic trim pieces—can actually mean two separate things. First, we have the chance of replacing the badge, emblem, nameplate, armrest base, etc. with a similar one (NOS, used or reproduction). Secondly, we have the hands-on job of taking the damaged emblem off the vehicle and attaching or installing another one. Both possibilities are worthy of discussion.

Given the cost and hassle of restoring a "chromed" plastic piece, the idea of swapping a bad one for a good one has great appeal. The ultimate fix is locating an NOS (new old stock) part to mount in place of the broken or worn one. Swap meet vendors, ads in hobby publications, and online auctions are the top three places to look for such never-used old parts.

Avoid purchasing pricey NOS parts based only on looking at them. There may be multiple sizes of Ford shield

Light scratching, as seen on this '89 Caprice door handle surround, is a common type of wear suffered by "chromed" plastic. Unfortunately, you can't buff this material like you can buff metal.

badges that all look alike, but don't fit exactly the same. Check a factory-issued master parts catalog or an aftermarket "crash book" to get the correct parts number. This number should be stamped on the part and printed on the box. However, since an incorrect part may be in a box, be sure to check the number on the part itself.

When searching for used chrome-plated plastic interior parts, remember that the same bezel or emblem may have been used on different models and different body styles. You might find it impossible to locate a used convertible part in good condition, but a part from a more weather-tight sedan may be identical. Keep in mind, too, that rare used parts with bad "plating"—but no other damage (like chips or cracks)—may be worth salvaging and restoring.

Reproduction parts are another possibility. So many old cars are being restored these days that the volume of reproduction parts being made is mind-boggling. Before you spend a ton of money for NOS parts or traveling to salvage

yards, make sure that a reproduction version of the part doesn't exist.

The actual replacement—or installation—of an NOS, good used or reproduction chrome plastic part can vary in its degree of difficulty. Badges, emblems, and nameplates will have plastic studs on the back that pass through mounting holes in the body. "Speed nuts" are usually used to hold them to the car. These are small tabs with a hole in the center and they twist right on to the plastic studs, biting slightly into the plastic stud to make their own light "threads." Be careful not to force anything or you might break the plastic stud.

Sometimes a plastic trim part, like a hubcap center, will be secured by tabs that you carefully bend outward to release the plastic piece. Special pliers do a good job of bending the tabs. After the emblem is swapped for a good one, carefully push the tabs back into place with a large flat-blade screwdriver.

Plastic armrest bases, console and dashboard trim, and seat plates may be secured by long screws. In many cases,

Special plastic polishes have advantages and limitations. This Caprice power door lock switch housing had ugly "plastic" chrome on the side and the front edge.

This plastic hubcap with imitation bright metal finish looked a bit sad after years on the shelf. The center section had light scratches on it. As you can see, it did not even bring $5 at a swap meet.

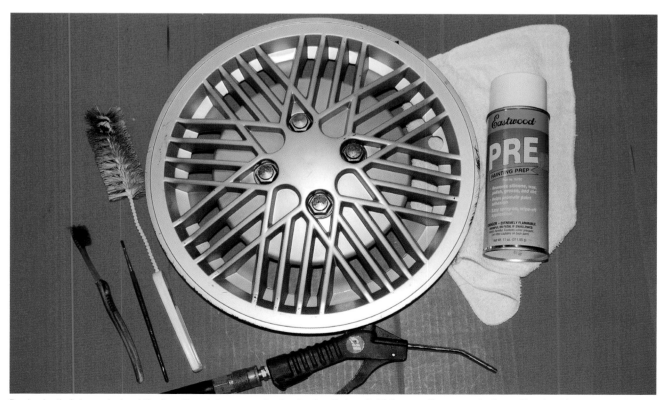

For cleaning the hubcap prior to painting it, you'll need clean rags and various brushes. Eastwood's P.R.E. spray will remove contaminants. Blow dry with compressed air. Before using P.R.E., test it on back to make sure it doesn't crinkle the silver paint.

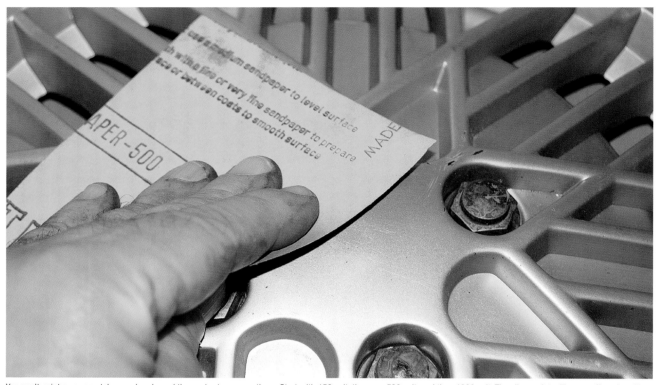

You can't paint away scratches, so hand-sand the center to remove them. Start with 150-grit, then use 500-grit, and then 1000-grit. The silver paint will come off, and you'll see traces of the black plastic underneath.

After sanding, use compressed air to blow every speck of sanding dust off the surface of the entire plastic hubcap. You can also spray some P.R.E. on a cotton rag and give the hubcap a final wiping off.

Hang the hubcap up and spray it. In this case, we hung it with a bungee cord and used duct tape to fasten cardboard behind it. We used a product that Eastwood sells called *Aervo* Chrome-Galvanized paint and it worked great.

these are installed so the screw heads are hidden from sight. They may screw into deep holes in an armrest base from below or there may be snap-in-place plastic covers to hide the screw heads.

REPAIR

Some hobbyists say it's impossible to restore chrome plastic, but it can be easily and affordably restored using a physical vapor deposition (PVD) process. This requires special equipment. As far as we know, there is no system designed to do this at home. The cost for "metalizing" a plastic armrest base is about $35.

It is possible to electroplate plastic, but this involves a difficult and costly process. At the Atlantic City Classic Car Auction and Swap Meet, we talked to Bill Wilds of Paul's Chrome Plating, whose company is now offering this service. The basics of this system are described later in this section.

A number of companies have PVD operations that offer vacuum metalizing to car restorers and model car builders. They start by washing parts in a chemical bath to strip off old finish and other contaminants. The bare plastic part is wet sanded to remove surface flaws and achieve a smooth surface. This is important, as the bright metal vapor can actually emphasize surface imperfections. Sanding the part promotes better adhesion of the vapor. If the part requires repairs or design improvements, these may be done at this point.

When the part is clean and sanded, a base coat is applied. This makes it even smoother and helps insure that the metalized finish will adhere well. Some companies use a urethane base coat, and others used a baked-on base coat.

The plastic parts are loaded into a vacuum chamber, where the plating process is carried out. All oxygen is evacuated from the chamber with a pump. Filaments are fired to evaporate the aluminum in the vacuum chamber. The aluminum vapor then condenses back onto the parts, bonding to them and forming a uniform coating of metal that looks like chrome.

After the parts are plated, a urethane clear coat similar to that used by the automakers is then applied to seal the chromelike finish. Then, the parts are baked once again to cure the paint. The part is then masked so that the back can be painted in the factory style. Any original factory markings can be restamped with the same kind of stamping machine the factory used when producing the part.

Never clean metalized parts with abrasive materials. Use only a damp, soft rag. Chemicals in household cleaners can turn the clear coat hazy or milky. Some vendors specifically state that they use clear coats not affected by household cleaners, so check all vendor ads or websites before choosing one.

The electroplating of chrome, as now offered by Paul's Chrome Plating, works a bit differently. The company actually encases a plastic part in copper before plating it. The part is stripped to bare plastic. Breaks or cracks in the part are fixed. Then, the plastic part is impregnated with silver so it conducts electricity. The part is then built up with copper, sanded, and buffed. A corrosion-resistant nickel-cobalt alloy is plated on the part and the part is then dipped in a

After spraying the hubcap with *Aervo* Chrome-Galvanized paint it looked like this. The center section was very smooth and was even shiny enough to slightly show our reflection in the painted surface. We could probably get our $5 for the hubcap now.

A simulated metallic Argent Silver finish is correct for the hood scoop on this '70 Hemi 'Cuda. For this application—worth big bucks, it would be best to use a spray gun, rather than a rattle can.

chrome-plating tank to apply the shiny finish. The cost for this special service varies according to the time the job takes. Basically, the cost is similar to that of pot metal restoration.

REFINISHING

In addition to a chromelike finish, physical vapor deposition—or metalizing—can be used to apply many other types of shiny finishes to plastic parts. The highly reflective coatings used in headlights and emergency flashers (such as first responders have in their cars) can be applied or restored via this process. The full range of possible finishes includes colored chrome, gold, bronze, and matte finishes. Custom chromelike coatings can also be applied to anything made of plastic, like a chrome steering wheel for a hot rod.

Hobbyists who are on a budget or simply fixing up a car, rather than doing a show restoration, might be very satisfied with the chromelike finishes they can achieve with special metallic paints.

Eastwood's Liquid Chrome allows the hobbyist to achieve a shiny surface that approaches the reflectivity of chrome. It is a paint that goes on over a smooth, glossy black urethane surface. You apply just a few light "mist" coats of Liquid Chrome, and follow up with the application of Eastwood's Liquid Chrome Clear. The product must be applied with a No. 5 tip or by use of a jamb/touch-up gun. At the time of writing, a Liquid Chrome and Clear Kit retailed for $69.99 and the Urethane Black and activator was $39.99 per quart. While not cheap, that is quite a bit of a saving over plating or metalizing if you do things right and get good results.

Eastwood's Almost Chrome is another do-it-at-home option. This is a spray-on paint that comes in a "rattle can" and looks almost like plating when used correctly. Eastwood says it is "reflective enough to faintly see yourself in it." It is approximately 30 percent as reflective as real chrome. It works well on underhood parts, chassis hardware, small brackets, and plastic interior parts. A 13-ounce aerosol can was $12.99 at the time of writing.

Chapter 10
Other Metal and Plastic Trim

For over 25 years, John Berry of Davenport, Iowa, painted and printed reproduction faces for antique motorcycle speedometers. In 1997, a Jaguar owner told John that the skills he used to restore gauges were in demand. Today, John's Phoenix Restoration restores gauges, trim plates, and body tags.

Cars have parts that we may not think of as "trim" that are really part of the vehicle's overall decorative treatment. For example, the shape, color, and style of lettering on your speedometer are a part of your car's design. To restore the car, you'll also have to restore a variety of "trim" parts made of metal and plastic. The metal parts include gauge faces, radio delete plates, dashboard panels, medallions,

etc. The plastic items include such things as inserts, emblems and console covers.

RESTORING METAL GAUGE FACES

While there are many stick-on overlays for popular antique auto gauges, John Berry prefers starting from scratch. Many overlays are the wrong color. Some reproductions are too glossy and others are simply not done well.

After disassembly, John does new artwork to match the original. This can be as simple as setting type that matches the original. Other letter styles can't be matched, so Berry calls on his sign painting experience to hand-paint masters. Later, he can convert these to silk screens and reprint the same faces.

This is a '38 Plymouth pickup truck speedometer before Phoenix Restoration repaired it. Owner John Berry hand-paints the gauge face design and then makes a silkscreen so that he can print it. *Phoenix Restoration*

Here is the '38 Plymouth pickup truck speedometer after being renewed by John Berry at Phoenix Restoration in Davenport, Iowa. Berry does the graphics and has a restorer who does the mechanicals. *Phoenix Restoration*

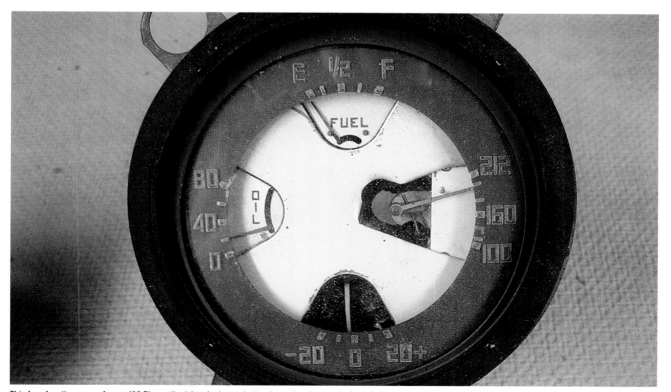

This four-function gauge from a '38 Plymouth pickup had seen better days when it came to Phoenix Restoration. In fact, someone had even replaced several of the original gauges with incorrect units. *Phoenix Restoration*

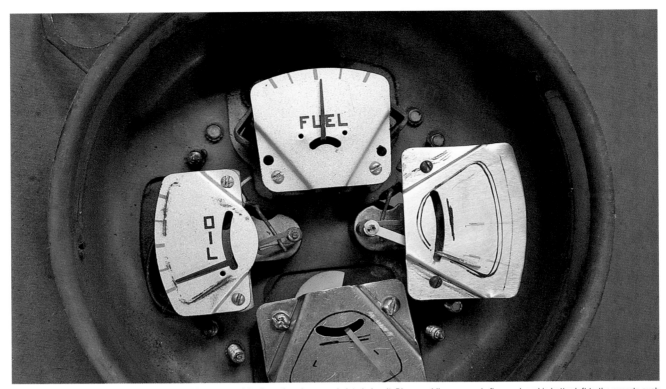

After removing the face from the '38 Plymouth pickup gauge, John Berry found a second plate below it. Disassembling gauges is fine work and is better left to the experts such as Phoenix Restoration. *Phoenix Restoration*

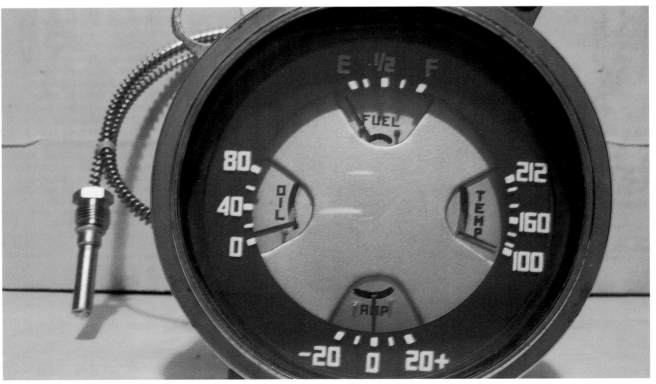

Here's the '38 Plymouth pickup gauge with the fuel level, oil pressure, ammeter, and temperature gauges all working perfectly and the face plate design restored. Note the new water temp sending unit. *Phoenix Restoration*

John takes care to match paint to the original face colors. He then strips the face of old paint. Some faces are made of brass with transparent glazes. These glazes are mixed prior to any stripping. John straightens the face, if necessary, and makes sure there's no rust. Some faces are beyond repair and have to be remade of aluminum or brass.

After that, it's a case of priming and repainting or reglazing. Again, silkscreens are made so that the faces can be reprinted and remounted to the gauges. The needles are painted the proper color, and the gauges are reinstalled.

RESTORING METAL PLATES, PANELS, MEDALLIONS, ETC.

John Berry recently restored a '38 Packard radio delete plate that had been hit with a hammer. The glass was completely gone, and the brass inner panels were badly bent up.

Since Packards were upscale cars, far more were produced with radios than without, making radio deletes difficult to find. Berry located a man with a still boxed NOS plate, plus another still in a car. The man would not consider selling either one, but let John photograph the one in the vehicle.

John hand-hammered new circular brass parts and glazed them to match the originals. He then took his photo of the original piece and used it to match the lettering style on the inner glass face. Berry drew on his 40-plus years as a sign painter and screen printer to hand-paint a master to match the lettering. He then made a silk screen and printed the lettering on the back side of new glass.

Berry replaced the curved glass outer face, cutting a piece from the center of a 12-inch curved-glass clock face. He replicated the plastic disk and hand-built and polished an aluminum trim ring. John mounted the refurbished original emblem and affixed everything to the center of the new delete panel. Luckily, the original chrome bezel was unharmed. It only needed a good cleaning.

PRESERVING EXISTING PLASTIC TRIM

"Plastic" is a term for synthetics. Plastic trim parts are found in cars of the 1930s on. To preserve the plastic trim, you must know what it is made of. *Natural* "plastics" include amber, horn, wax, shellac, and rubber. *Semisynthetics* are chemically modified natural materials like ebonite and vulcanite. *Full synthetics* include Bakelite and "poly" plastics like Lucite and polyurethane.

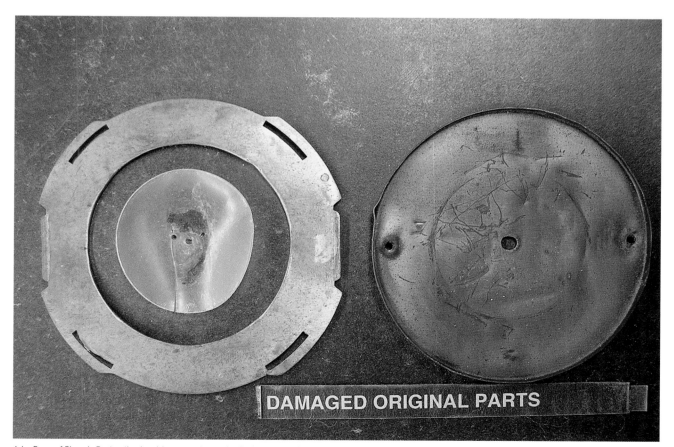

DAMAGED ORIGINAL PARTS

John Berry of Phoenix Restoration hand-hammered new circular brass parts for the battered Packard radio delete plate. John glazed his reproductions to match these damaged original parts. *Phoenix Restoration*

Berry photographed all pieces of the Packard plate. After 40-plus years of painting and screen-printing, he knows how to paint a master to match lettering. He duplicated the lettering on the inner glass face. *Phoenix Restoration*

You are not going to test car parts, so you'll rely on age, appearance, feel, smell, and properties to identify the plastic in your car. Bakelite is a hard, dark 1940s material with a carbolic smell. Polyvinyl chloride is a clear or yellowish 1940s material with a plasticizer smell. Casein plastic is a hard, light-colored material used from 1910 to 1930. Cellulose acetate, used from 1930 to 1950, has a vinegary smell. Imitation tortoiseshell is cellulose nitrate and smells of camphor. Polystyrene, used in the 1940s and 1950s, is hard and brightly colored.

Plastic was once viewed as virtually impervious to degradation—a material that could last forever. Unfortunately for automobile collectors, that perception is not true. Each type of plastic suffers different problems as it ages. PVC loses its plasticisers, resulting in a sticky surface that attracts dirt. It also hardens, causing cracks and yellowing. Physical and environmental stresses crack and split Casein plastic. Steps can be taken to offset deterioration.

Cleaning and Storing

Brushing and dusting is the best way to clean plastic. Slightly damp cotton swabs work, but make sure the water is thoroughly dried off afterward.

Storing plastics at low temperature and relative humidity will slow down the rate of degradation. Shielding plastic from sunlight and artificial light preserves it. A car cover will help plastic trim parts last longer.

Storing the vehicle in a cool, dry environment will help to preserve its plastic trim parts. Never store plastic parts taken off a car in humid surroundings, such as laundry rooms, as this can warp them.

Plastic that's degrading may affect nearby plastic parts that are good. One thing you can do is loosely cover the deteriorating plastic parts with acid-free tissue or silicone paper when not using the car. This will also keep them free of dirt. If you spot surface acid, you can remove it with a dry or very lightly moistened tissue. Keep the tissue from sticking and remove all moisture later.

John Berry also restores old license plates. If you live in a state that allows collector cars to be operated with year of manufacture (YOM) plates, the old license plates actually become part of your car's "trim."

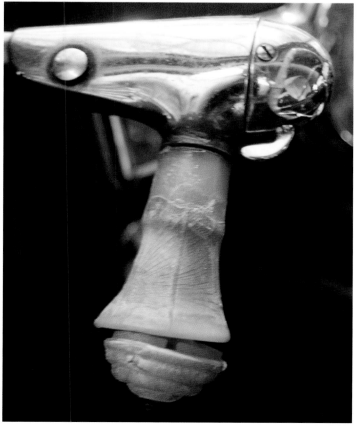

The old types of plastic used in the late 1930s and throughout the 1940s often do not age well. This is the handle on a windshield spotlight that is mounted on the author's '48 Pontiac Streamliner. Isn't it ugly?

The numbers and markings on this speedometer face are certainly showing their age. Restorations of this type are beyond the capabilities of the typical do-it-yourselfer. *Auto Instruments Corp.*

An important part of the restoration process at Auto Instruments is to carefully sandblast the face. This will allow proper adhesion of the new paint and graphics. *Auto Instruments Corp.*

Chemical Dos and Don'ts

Chemicals can damage plastic trim parts. Different chemicals affect the strength, flexibility, appearance, dimensions, and weight of plastics, depending on length of exposure, temperature, and concentration. The use of certain fluids—like household detergents, lubricants, oils, surface additives, or even pure water—combined with physical and environmental stresses, can crack and split old plastic. Prolonged exposure to strong oxidizing agents can make plastic brittle.

Generally, you can clean most plastic car parts with special detergents and rinse them with distilled water. Avoid using scourers or abrasive cleaners.

It's not a good idea to rub any type of cleaner or polish on plastic, unless its manufacturer specifically recommends it for plastic. Read the instructions. Most manufacturers will recommend cleaning the part with an automotive soap and water mixture first. This can be followed by a clean water rinse.

Meguiar's sells a Plastx Clear Plastic Cleaner & Polish. It does an acceptable job of cleaning plastic parts. This polish relies on modern micro abrasive technology. It provides a powerful, but safe, cleaning and polishing action. The nontoxic polish contains no harsh solvents.

REPLACING DAMAGED PLASTIC TRIM

If you're lucky, you can replace your car's damaged plastic trim with NOS, used, or reproduction parts. The newer the car, the easier to find replacements.

To remove plastic trim parts, you may have to use a single-edge razor or a Dremel tool to trim studs and split-ball snap-in holders. In other cases, plastic edge tabs will have to be pried. Dental picks and a set of Eastwood's plastic pry tools will help in removing plastic trim.

If you're replacing glued-on plastic trim, a chemical gum-and-adhesive remover or a heat gun may help. Just remember that chemicals and heat can ruin plastic parts, so you must try to soften the glue without harming the plastic. If you must touch the plastic with a chemical or heat, test with a scrap piece first.

The finished product is a perfect reproduction of the long suffering original, with sharp, crisp lines and numerals. It will be the ideal finishing touch for the interior in which it is about to be reinstalled. *Auto Instruments Corp.*

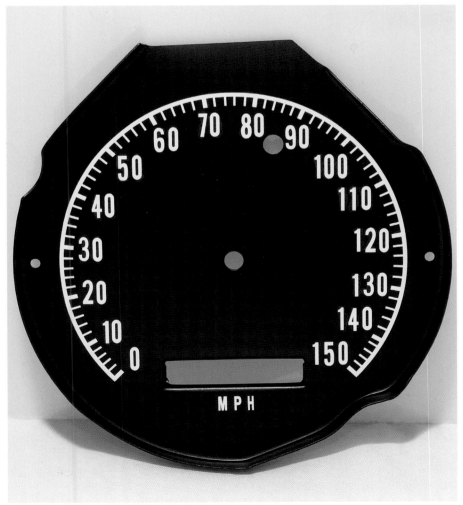

Brought to you by the same '48 Pontiac, here's an example of typical deterioration in the plastic steering wheel rims of 60 years ago. Classic Plus Ltd. (see Appendix) does awesome steering wheel restorations.

REPAIRING DAMAGED PLASTIC TRIM

Years ago, restorers simply threw away damaged plastic trim and went to a salvage yard for a new piece. Today there are few salvage yards left and most of the old cars remaining in them do not have a salvageable piece of plastic trim.

You may find old plastic trim that can be repaired. Methods of "welding" cracks in plastic have been developed. Plastic that's turned milky or cloudy by humidity or bad weather can sometimes be polished and restored. Broken mounting studs can be repaired. After such repairs, the trim can be refinished. Finally, it is possible for a restorer to cast plastic parts to replace originals.

Crack Repairs

Plastic welding can fix cracks in plastic trim. Discount tool suppliers sell plastic welders. As in regular welding, success will rely on good joint preparation, correct heat and air pressure, having the proper filler, and tip selection.

You need to know the type of plastic and its welding requirements. Thermoset plastics are difficult to weld. Thermoplastics weld easier. Heat and pressure requirements vary. Rods should be of the same material you're welding. Be sure to use the right tip.

Plastic welding requires the simultaneous and equal heating of the piece, weld rod, and weld bed by the welding

If you really want to enhance the looks of your car's interior, you can polish and clean old plastic parts—like this '48 Pontiac radio volume knob—and finish them with a light coat of clear.

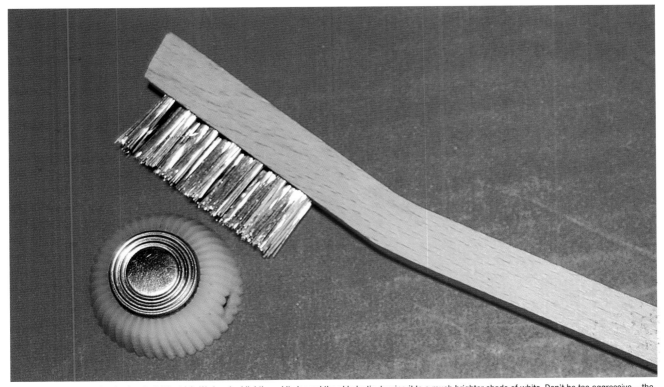

A stainless-steel parts cleaning brush did the trick. We brushed lightly and it cleaned the old plastic, turning it to a much brighter shade of white. Don't be too aggressive—the bristles can bite. You want it smooth.

We used fine 400- and then 600-grit black sandpaper to give a shine to the metal center without scratching it up. You can lightly rub the center into the sandpaper or tear off a small piece and work with that.

Chris Daniels, of Indian Bonnet, in Mooresville, North Carolina, couldn't find a correct Indian head for his '48 Indian motorcycle for under $500. He went to a firm that sells resins. They taught him how to make molds.

gun's hot gas stream. You control the heat by moving the tip toward or away from the piece. If you do things right, you'll wind up with a nice homogeneous bead and a good repair.

Repairing Environmental Damage

Polishing repairs environmental damage to plastic trim parts. Years ago, Don Barlup, of Camphill, Pennsylvania, purchased a Plexiglas-bodied Pontiac that was built for the 1939–1940 New York World's Fair. When he first got the car, the see-through plastic body was milky and cloudy. A Pontiac dealer offered to restore it by polishing the Plexiglas. He was able to make the car look much like it did three decades earlier.

The Meguiar's Plastx Clear Plastic Cleaner & Polish mentioned earlier was used in a *Bike World* test of products for cleaning and polishing plastic motorcycle windscreens. Plastx utilizes nanotechnology that makes it suitable for removing fine scratches, oxidation, grime, haze, and cloudiness from plastic. *Bike World* said it was not the best bug remover, but it did an exceptional job repairing the environmental damage that restorers deal with.

Fixing Broken Attachments

Pins, studs, tabs, and tangs that attach plastic trim parts to cars can break. If you think you will never have to remove the piece again, the easiest fix may be using a two-part epoxy to glue it in place. Before making a permanent attachment like this, be sure it doesn't have to be removed to gain access to other parts.

Pins and studs can be fixed using a small drill in a Dremel tool. Be careful not to drill all the way through the plastic. A two-part epoxy will hold the new pin or stud in place. If the original stud came out of a raised boss, clean the original hole, and screw in a small bolt to replace the stud. Hacksaw the head off the bolt.

Broken plastic tabs or tangs are a nuisance. You can epoxy new ones on, but they are usually under stress and will soon break again. We have had fairly good luck replacing the broken tabs with metal clips. These may be separate, or sometimes it's possible to attach them permanently with plastic welding.

Seen here is a one-piece reproduction with features that are too smooth. Chris' more detailed reproduction is made from a two-part resin. It is an exact copy of the original two-piece Indian head and sells for $50.

The non-original-style reproduction on the left has smooth facial features and no seam. While very nice looking, it is not as true to the original design as Chris Daniel's "Indian Bonnet" reproduction on the right.

REFINISHING DAMAGED PLASTIC TRIM

Plastic trim parts that you fix can be refinished using a variety of methods discussed earlier in the book. Plastic chrome is one option. They can also be painted with specially formulated paints. Water transfer printing can also be done on plastic parts. This would be particularly good for restoring trim parts with grained, marbleized, simulated engine-turned, or carbon weave finishes.

FABRICATING PLASTIC TRIM REPLACEMENTS

Chris Daniels, of Indian Bonnet, in Mooresville, North Carolina., manufactures resin-cast Indian faces for 1947–1953 Indian motorcycles. He showed us a factory-style, two-piece casting he makes and compared it to a cheap one-piece casting.

Chris couldn't find an original Indian head for the bonnet on his own 1948 Indian Chief for less than $500. He decided to go to a company that sells resins, and they taught him how to make molds. He uses a two-part resin to make exact replicas of the original part and sells them for $50.

"The cheap reproduction is too white, too smooth, and doesn't have a seam like the original," Chris explained. "They made it that way because it's easier, when casting resin, to avoid using a double mold like I do." Daniel's fender mascots have the same sharp details the factory originals do.

Companies that have equipment to spin cast plastic parts can also reproduce vintage car parts. Spin casting was developed as an inexpensive way for manufacturers to have prototypes of parts made. At least one company that does spin casting has made parts for an auto restorer.

Chapter 11
Helpful Modern Coating Methods

When restoring trim parts on a collector car, several newer methods of top coating metal may prove handy. Powder coating, invented in Australia in the late 1960s, is a way of applying dry paint to a part and using heat to cure it. E-coating is a type of painting using electrical current to deposit the paint. Rust-preventative paints are brushed- or sprayed-on coatings that seal metal from oxidation-causing air. Ceramic paints are an exciting new product for restorers.

Both amateur and professional restorers can do powder coating. Eastwood and other firms sell systems aimed at the home restorer. For high-volume production work or larger parts, larger, heavier-duty equipment is needed. Commercial powder coaters can be found throughout the United States.

Powder coating is popular in the hot rod, custom car, and custom motorcycle hobbies. Restorers seem to have mixed feelings, because it was not originally used on the cars they now restore. In certain clubs and venues, points may be deducted, in judged car shows, for powder coating. However, the process is very well suited to metal trim restoration work.

When restoring trim parts on a collector car, several newer methods of top coating metal may come in handy. Here's a sampling of paint colors offered from just one company that supplies restorers—Eastwood. *Eastwood*

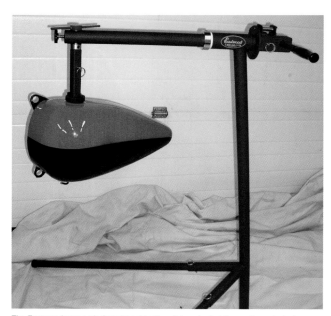

The Eastwood research department tests a fixture for holding motorcycle tanks during painting or powder coating. Powder coating is popular on custom bikes and is catching on more and more with car restorers.

Powder coating can give enamel-like effects on colored emblems and badges. It can also provide a top coat that looks very much like chrome plating. We have seen toy cars with "chrome grilles" done with powder coating and they looked great. Body side moldings that have indented areas painted could also be powder coated and the contrasting color would virtually last forever.

E-coatings are used in industrial production to give metal a durable finish. Certain types of trim parts—especially any finished with black or galvanized finishes—would benefit greatly from the use of long-lasting E-coats.

Rust-preventative paints generally wouldn't be used on trim. However, they may be a natural for treating the metal *under* the trim to keep it from rusting. As we all know, when holes are drilled to attach bright metal trim to a car, it exposes bare metal. That bare steel will quickly start rusting if not quickly protected. Rust-preventative paints can be brushed or sprayed on both sides of such holes to prevent the rapid formation of oxidation.

Ceramic paints are virtually brand-new. They hit the market only a few months ago and promise to have many useful applications.

Newly developed multistage ceramic paints promise home restorers a big plus in refinishing chassis parts. Innovators are sure to start testing whether they have any advantages in the restoration of trim parts. *Eastwood*

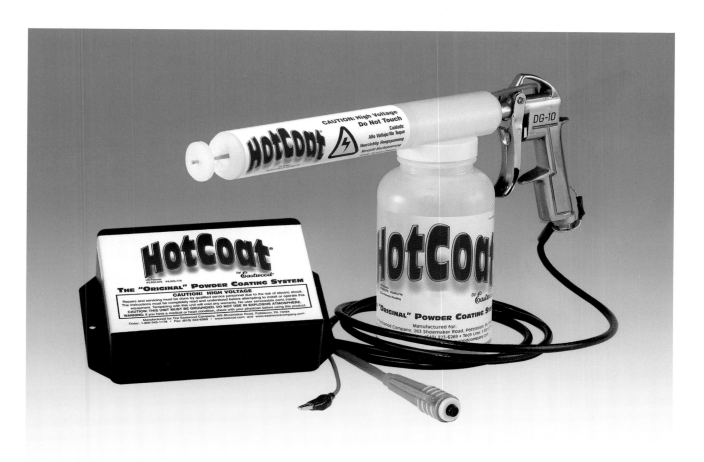

Hot Coat products and similar systems have been created to allow hobbyists to powder coat parts at home. Basic kits have been developed to get shade tree mechanics into powder coating for under $100. *Eastwood*

POWDER COATING

With regular paint, solid pigments are suspended in a liquid that evaporates, leaving the painted surface with a top coat. With powder coating, a colored powder is applied to the surface and heat-cured. During the curing, chemical cross-linking occurs. This makes powder coated parts look very good.

Powder coaters may use a *thermoplastic* powder that remelts when heated or a *thermosetting* powder that doesn't remelt. There are two ways to apply the powder. In the first, the item is lowered into a fluidized bed of the powder, which is or isn't electrostatically charged. In method two, the powdered paint is electrostatically charged and sprayed onto the part. The powered part then goes into an oven that melts the powder, forming a smooth, continuous film.

Successful powder coating requires careful preparation of the part. Contaminants on the part could keep spots from accepting the powder. This would create pores in the coating through which rust could start. Surface preparation treatments vary according to the metal being powder coated. Home powder coating kits include surface preparation instructions.

Powder coaters use weak alkali or neutral detergent solutions to remove oil and grease. The surface is then etched to remove heavy oxides. After rinsing, the metal is dipped into a solution that creates a conversion coating. The powder is applied with an electrostatic spray gun. Since the powder is electrostatically charged, it clings to the part. The powder remains there as long as it's charged.

Next, the powder coated items are placed in an oven and heated to temperatures between 160 to 210 degrees Celsius. The thermo-setting powder goes through four steps—melting, flowing, gelling, and curing. The powder coat is continuous. It will vary from high gloss to matt finish, depending on the powder.

Different types of powder coating guns are used to create the electrostatic charge in different ways. Corona charging guns use electric power. Tribo charging guns use friction between the gun and powder. Bell charging guns rely on dispersion of the powder from the outside of a bell.

The hobbyist can use a safe old kitchen oven for curing the powder, if the parts being coated fit inside. Eastwood and other suppliers also sell single- and dual-head curing

No wonder motorcycle builders like powder coating. This engine, created by a company called Diamond Heads, is done with an attractive yellow powder coat that looks great and won't chip or wear off. *Eastwood*

lamps for home restorers who can't justify the cost of a large curing oven. If used carefully and skillfully, the lamps give professional results.

Smoothness, hardness, and durability are big selling points for powder coating, but trim restorers will be more interested in different effects powder coating can give. An almost endless array of colors and finishes is available.

E-COATINGS

E-coatings are applied using an electrical current to deposit paint on a part. This is known as the electrodeposition of a top coating. E-coating cannot be carried out by the home restorer. However, it would be very useful in the finishing of painted trim parts that a parts supplier mass-produces for collector cars. For example, someone manufacturing flat black exterior trim pieces for a 1960s muscle car might go for the superior durability that E-coat finishes would provide.

Before a surface can be E-coated, it must be cleaned and treated with a phosphate material. A zinc phosphate treatment is best for iron and steel parts. Different treatments are required for other metals, such as aluminum.

An E-coating is applied in an electrocoat bath consisting of 80–90 percent deionized water and 10–20 percent paint solids. The deionized water carries the paint solids (resin and pigment). These solids are constantly agitated all the time the E-coating process is going on. The resin provides corrosion protection, durability, and toughness. The pigment provides the color and glossiness.

During E-coating, paint is applied to a part at a specific film thickness, which is controlled by the voltage. When proper thickness is achieved, the part insulates and the coating process slows down. As the part leaves the bath, paint solids stick to its surface. These must be rinsed off. The residue or cream coat is put back in the tank, making the system 95 percent efficient.

After being rinsed, the part enters a bake oven that cross-links the molecules and cures the paint film. The part is baked for at least 20 minutes at a minimum of 375 degrees. Low-temperature cures do exist for E-coatings that are used on mechanical parts with rubber seals, bushings, or bearings.

There are different types of E-coats. Cathodic epoxy E-coats provide good adhesion and corrosion protection.

Before applying rust-resistant finishes, the metal that is being finished should be treated with Eastwood's Fast Etch Acid Base Rust Remover and their Metal Prep or comparable products. *Eastwood*

Go to a salvage yard and yank an unrestorable molding off an old car. You'll see an outline of the molding on the car. In 9 out of 10 instances, the outline has surface rust. You'll usually find rusty clips, too. *Jesse Gunnell*

Gear up when spraying paint, like this restorer applying multistage ceramic paint to a chassis. Modern finishes have tricky chemical makeups. Personal protection equipment (PPE) could save your life.

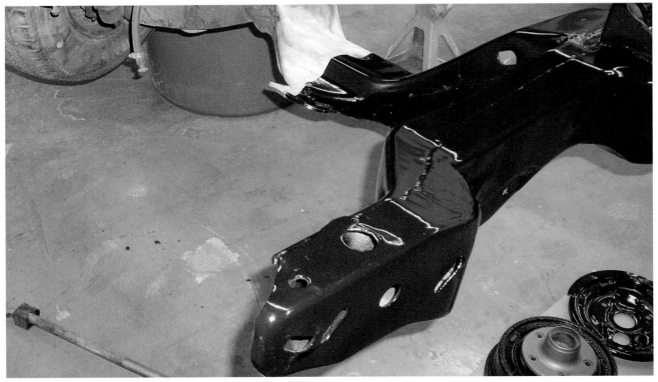

Ceramic paint comes in satin and high-gloss formulas. The high-gloss has an especially nice, extremely hard sheen, almost like an enameled trim badge.

They are compatible with many liquid and powder top coats. They are for parts where a cure temperature above 380 degrees Fahrenheit is possible. Anodic epoxy E-coats provide better adhesion and corrosion resistance than paint and can be cured at temperatures as low as 180°F. Cathodic acrylic E-coats resist ultraviolet rays, even in single-stage applications.

E-coatings are generally restricted to a single color. If additional color options are required, the cathodic acrylic E-coat can serve as the primary color, or it can be used as a primer that is top coated with a liquid or powder finish.

RUST PREVENTATIVE PAINTS

Tried-and-trusted Rustoleum paints, a variety of POR-15 products, and Eastwood's Rust Encapsulator are the best-known rust-preventative paints. The idea behind all of these products is to apply a finish that seals a metal surface from moisture and air so that oxidation will not continue after the surface is painted. Eastwood also has a new product called Heavy-Duty Anti Rust that leaves a waxy, oily coating that has certain advantages and certain restrictions.

Heavy-Duty Anti Rust resists cracking and peeling and is self-healing if it gets scratched. It gives very durable rust protection to metal, but since it is waxy and oily and can't be painted over, it is best for use on internal surfaces such as a rocker panel, a tailgate, or the inside of a fender or door.

None of these products are really designed to be used to apply an automotive top coat, so their use in restoring automotive trim pieces would be very limited, at best. However, all of them can be used on the back of a metal trim piece to keep it from rusting or discoloring the body panel it's ultimately attached to. Better yet, these products can all be used to fight off one of the biggest problems caused by the ways in which trim was mounted in the old days.

Gardner-Westcott Co. of Northville, Michigan, is one of several companies that prepackage bolt and hardware kits for specific models of cars and motorcycles. *Eastwood*

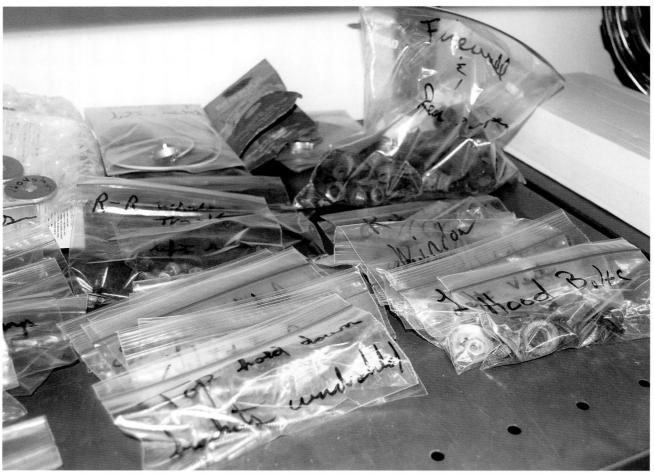

It is very important to save every fastener, broken or not, that you find as you take a car apart. Restorer Jerry Kopecky stores them in baggies and carefully labels each "bag of bolts" with a black marker pen.

If you go to a salvage yard and yank an unrestorable trim molding off an old car, you'll see an outline of the molding remaining on the car. In nine out of 10 instances, the outline will show surface rust, rather than just dirt. You will usually find extremely rusty clips and screws that held the molding to the body.

The holes that factory workers drilled in the door or fender to accept the clips and screws will likely be blistered by heavy corrosion. The rust will be pushing flakes of paint off the body where it surrounds the holes. The body panel may even have rust-through caused by the corrosive action that began when the holes were drilled, which of course removed paint and exposed bare metal.

After you've finished restoring the car, why not take steps to prevent the same thing from happening? When you repainted the body, the holes were there and finally got painted, but attaching trim may scrape some off again. A little Heavy-Duty Anti Rust around the holes will self-cure if scratched. You could also paint the entire inside of the door with this product. And why not use a rust-preventative paint on the back of the molding itself, as well as the screws and clips you use to attach it? A few of these paints come in clear, silver, or gray colors, which might be best in these particular applications. A black paint might show up slightly on the edges of the molding and give a nonfactory look.

CERAMIC PAINT

Eastwood's new 2K Ceramic Chassis Black is made for painting frames. It is blended with finely ground ceramic particles. These produce a chip- and chemical-resistant coating that could come in very handy for touching up color accents on badges, emblems, moldings, trim plates, and other bright metal parts. It could also be used to refinish black trim parts.

As in any painting, Eastwood's PRE—or a similar product—should be applied to remove dirt, wax, and grease. Next, cover the cleaned part with a high-quality primer. Eastwood recommends its own Epoxy 1:1 Gray Primer. This might be wise, since it is considered a good idea to stay in the same product "family."

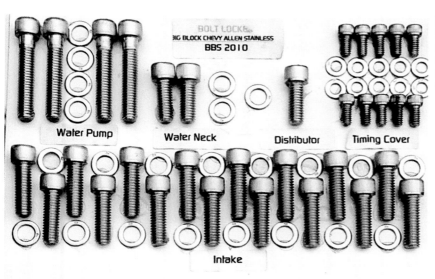

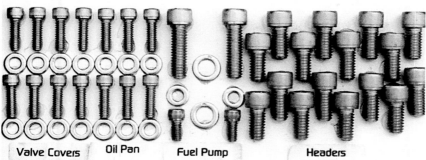

When restoring a car, companies like Bolt Locker (www.boltlocker.com) of Eau Claire, Wisconsin, can help you replace the old fasteners on your car with hardware kits custom-selected for different models of cars or different engines. They offer a choice of cadmium-plated steel or stainless steel.

A high-torque motor is used to make this heavy-duty tumbler vibrate. With its tumbling action, the Metal Clean media in the tumbler abrades the hardware placed inside and cleans it of dirt, oil, and grease. *Eastwood*

This media screen is a heavy plastic sifter and catch pan with a ⅜-x ¾-inch mesh. This one costs under $25 and comes in handy when cleaning old car hardware. *Eastwood*

Eastwood's Metal Blackening System lets you apply OEM finishes to hardware in your home shop. *Eastwood*

When the primer dries, you can mix up the 2K Ceramic Chassis Black, which comes in a quart can, with eight ounces of Eastwood's 4:1 Urethane Activator. Then, start spraying. Despite containing ceramic particles, which give it its rugged characteristics, the ceramic paint sprays consistently from an HVLP (high volume low pressure) spray gun with a 1.5 to 1.7 tip.

You'll have to mask the trim piece, so that only the color fields or painted molding indentations receive color. The new finish is fast drying, so you won't have time to wipe off paint from areas that aren't supposed to be painted, as you did with regular paints.

The 2K Ceramic Chassis Black comes with a glossy or satin finish. The gloss finish would be suitable for finishing badges and emblems with black accents. The satin finish would work well on black metal trim for 1960s and 1970s cars. The ceramic particles in this product give it properties that resist chipping and chemicals. Chipping, of course, always seemed to be a big problem with old car emblems and badges that were battered by everything from acid rain to factory smoke. The 2K Ceramic Chassis Black also provides incredible resistance to the sun's ultraviolet rays and will stand up well outside your garage.

An expert in restoring the '57 Chevy, Steve Hamilton has studied every bolt and fastener on that particular model and keeps each piece in inventory. Steve never has to stop working due to a missing bolt.

Steve Hamilton keeps each type of bolt used on the '57 Chevy in a separate drawer of this sturdy old storage unit. When he does a car, every nut and bolt and hose clamp are the factory style parts.

Appendix

SUPPLIES AND SERVICES

Metalworking is the process of working with metals to form parts, assemblies, or structures.

SUPPLIES

Coatings

Central Mass Powder Coating
32 Greeley St.
Clinton, MA 01510
978-365-1700
www.CentralMassPowderCoating.com

Bill Hirsch
396 Littleton Ave.
Newark, NJ 07103
800-828-2061 or 973-642-2404
www.hirschauto.com

M+M Custom Finishing
9318 Corneits Rd.
Bristol, IL 60512
630-553-3143
www.mmcustomfinishing.com

Miller's Powder Coating
4251-B Wayside Ct.
Lilburn, GA 30047
770-931-1505
www.millerpowdercoating.com

Next Generation
170 Lockhouse Rd.
Westfield, MA 01085
413-562-4700
www.nextgenerationpowdercoating.com

Peacock Laboratories
PC Chrome
1901 S. 54th St.
Philadelphia, PA 19143
215-729-4400
www.Pchrome.com

PM Industries
800-833-8933
www.nomorerust.com

POR-15
PO Box 1235
Morristown, NJ 07962
800-726-0468
www.por15.com

Bob Young
New Jersey
973-927-0637

Hardware

Auto Hardware Specialties
3123 McKinley Ave.
Sheldon, IA 51201
712-326-2091

Bolt Locker
800 Wisconsin St.
Eau Claire, WI 54703
715-839-0556
www.boltlocker.com

Gardner-Westcott Co.
10110 Six Mile Rd.
Northville, MI 482167
248-305-5100 or 800-897-5025
www.gardner-westcott.com

Mr. G's Enterprises
5613 Elliott Reeder Rd.
Fort Worth, TX 76117
817-831-3501
www.mrgusa.com

Restoration Specialties & Supply, Inc.
PO Box 328
Windber, PA 15963
814-467-9842
www.restorationspecialties.com

Restoration Supply Co.
15182-B Highland Valley Rd.
Escondido, CA 92025
800-306-7008
www.restorationstuff.com

Totally Stainless
PO Box 3249
Gettysburg, PA 17325
800-767-4781 or 717-677-8811
www.totallystainless.com

Polishes

Kreem Products
105F Stonebrook Pl.
Suite 316
Jackson, TN 38305
731-506-4181
www.kreemproducts.net

Luster Lace Polishes
104 Trade Center Dr.
St. Peters, MO 63376
636-272-1885
www.lusterlace.com

Pot Metal Repair Supplies

Caswell Electroplating
7696 Route 31
Lyons, NY 14489
315-946-1213
www.caswellplating.com

Muggyweld
360-357-4770 or 866-684-4993
www.muggyweld.com

Tools

The Eastwood Company
263 Shoemaker Rd.
Pottstown, PA 19464
610-323-2200 or 800-343-9353
www.eastwood.com

Harbor Freight
3491 Mission Oaks Blvd.
Camarillo, CA 93011-6010
www.harborfreightusa.com

Lefthander Chassis
13750 Metric Dr.
Roscoe, IL 61073
815-389-9999
www.lefthanderchassis.com

Lincoln Electric
115 E. Crossroads Parkway
Suite A
Bolingbrook, IL 60440-3538
630-783-3600 or 773-412-5153
www.lincolnelectric.com

Mittler Brothers Machine and Tool
10 Cooperative Way
Wright City, MO 63390
636-745-7757
www.mittlerbros.com

Northern Tool + Equipment
PO Box 1499
Burnsville, MN 55306
800-221-5381
www.northerntool.com

Park Tool
6 Long Lake Rd.
St. Paul, MN 55115
651-777-6868
www.parktool.com

Performance Metal Shaping
(Martin Autobody Tools)
449 Hayward St.
Manchester, NH 03013
603-669-1475
www.performancemetalshaping.com

Woodward Fabrication
PO Box 425
1480 Old US 23
Hartland, MI 48353
800-391-5419
www.woodwardfab.com

Woodgraining Supplies
GIT Technologies, Inc.
334 Commerce Court
Winter Haven, FL 33880
863-299-4494
www.woodgraining.com

SERVICES
Bright Metal Trim Restoration
California Polishing
714-847-2166
www.californiapolishing.com

Classics Plus Ltd.
601 Lakeshore Dr.
N. Fond du Lac, WI 54937
888-923-1007
www.classicsplusltd.com

Custom Plating Specialist, Inc.
W797 County Road K
Brillion, WI 54110
920-756-3284
www.customplatingspecialists.com

Glassworks: The Hardtop Shop
113 McGovern Blvd
Crescent, PA 15046
724-457-0680
www.thehardtopshop.com

Iverson Automotive
14704 Karyl Dr.
Minnetonka, MN 55345
800-325-0480
www.iversonautomotive.com

MCB Performance Center
14500 Folley Rd.
Capac, MI 48014
810-543-0088 or 810-395-7162
www.tuffwheelrestoration.com

Vintage Vehicles Co.
N-1940 20th Dr.
Wautoma. WI 54982
920-787-2656
www.vintagevehicles.net

Bud Ward's Antique Cars
13001 Interstate 30
Little Rock, AR 72209
888-860-9664 or 501-455-1141
www.budwardsantiquecars.com

Bumper Restoration
Advanced Plating, Inc.
1425 Cowan Ct.
Nashville, TN 37207
800-588-6686
www.advancedplating.com

The Bumper Boyz
2435 E. 54th St.
Los Angeles, CA 90058
800-995-1703
www.bumperboyz.com

Custom Plating
3030 Alta Ridge Way
Snellville, GA 30078
770-736-1118

Fond du Lac Bumper Exchange
1285 Morris St.
Fond du Lac, WI 54935
800-236-2570 or 920-921-2570
www.fdlbumper.com

North Star Bumper Exchange
5085 Wren Dr.
Appleton, WI 54913
920-731-3030

Restoration Chrome
908 N. Lake Road
Spokane, WA 99212
509-534-0456
www.restorationchrome.com

Casting Repairs
A & C Casting Rebuilders
3560 Big Valley Rd. Unit A
Kelseyville, CA 95451
866-935-3227 or 707-278-0223
www.accastingrebuilders.com

Casting Salvage Technologies
Virginia
800-833-8814

Jon W. Gateman & Son
PO Box 413
Beatty, NV 89003
775-764-0976

Polish This, Inc
Jeff Goodhart
Leesport, PA
484-269-9450
www.polish-this.com

Lite Metals Company, Inc
7100 North Walnut St.
Ravenna, OH 44266
330-296-6110
www.litemetals.com

Ohio Pattern
614-875-9599

Emblem and Cloisonné Restoration
Allan Haywood Enamels
5 Montgomery St.
Skipton, 3361 Australia
+61 (0) 353402265
http://heywoodenamels.com

Emblemagic
PO Box 420
Grand River, OH 44045-0420
440-209-0792
www.emblemagic.com

Gauge Face Restorations
Nisonger Instruments
225 Hoyt Ave.
Mamaroneck, NY 10543
914-381-1952
www.nisongerinstruments.com

Phoenix Restoration
PO Box 458
Davenport, IA 52805
563-326-5144
www.phoenixresto.com

Metal Fabrication
Bennett Coachworks LLC
1500 North 4th St.
Milwaukee, WI 53212
414-298-2068
www.hotrodbuilders.com

Hamilton Classics
W4271 Ledge Rd.
Fond du Lac, WI 54935
920-924-9000 or 920-960-3619

Kopecky's Klassics
PO Box 473
N6871 Highway 49
Iola, WI 54945
715-445-4791 or 920-572-7942
www.kopeckysklassics.com

L'Cars Automotive Specialties
110 Poplar Ave.
PO Box 324
Cameron, WI 54822
715-458-2277
www.lcars.com

Precision Welding & Repair
E2235 King Rd.
Waupaca, WI 54981
715-258-5405

Frank Laiacano Jr.
29120 Badett
Westland, MI 48185
H-734-522-0797
B-734-425-9302
C-734-377-1825
classicparts4U@aol.com

Mirror Resilvering
Cliff's Classic Chevrolet Parts
619 SE 202nd Ave.
Portland, OR 97233
503-667-4329
www.cliffsclassicchevrolet.net

Reflective Image
21 West Wind Dr.
Northford, CT 06472
203-484-0760

Ron's Corner
27169 State Hwy 6
Winston, MO 64689
660-749-5473

Steve's Auto Restorations
4440 SE 174th Ave.
Portland, OR 97236-1381
503-665-2222
www.stevesautorestorations.com

Plating
A & A Plating
9400 E. Wilson Rd.
Independence. MO 64053
800-747-9914
www.aaplating.com

Advanced Plating & Powder Coating
1425 Cowan Ct.
Nashville, TN 37207
800-588-6686
www.advanceedplating.com

All-Brite Metal
2148 E. Tucker St.
Philadelphia, PA 19125
215-423-2234 or 267-872-0935

Charger Metals
2127 Margaret St.
Philadelphia, PA 19124
215-289-9227

Chrome Company, Inc.
630-543-5252
www.chrome.com

Custom Plating Specialists
W797 County Road K
Brillion, WI 54110
920-756-3284
http://customplatingspecialists.com

Detail Plating
2496 N. Zediker Ave.
Sanger, CA 93657
559-875-0290
www.detailplating.com

Graves Plating
4230 Chisholm Rd.
Florence, AL 35630
256-764-9487
www.gravesplating.com

Hanlon Plating Co.
925 East 4th St.
Richmond, VA 23224
804-233-2021
www.hanlonplating.com

J & P Custom Plating, Inc.
PO Box 16
807 N. Meridian St.
Portland, IN 47371
260-726-9696
www.jpcustomplating.com

Lakeside Custom Plating, Inc.
373 Commerce St.
Conneaut, OH 44030
440-599-2035
www.customchromerestoration.com

N.E.L. Metal Restorations
2127-35 Margaret St.
Philadelphia, PA 19124
215-289-4944
www.precisionchrome.com

Nu-Chrome
161 Graham Rd.
Fall River, MA 02720
800-422-8012
www.nu-chrome.com

Bill Oldenburg
4426 N. Sullivan La.
Galena, IL 61036
815-777-9204

Paul's Chrome Plating, Inc.
90 Pattison St.
Evans City, PA 16033
800-245-8679
www.paulschrome.com

Professional Plating, Inc.
705 Northway Dr.
Brillion, WI 54110
920-756-2153}
www.proplating.com

Speed & Sport Chrome Plating
404 Broadway St.
Houston, TX 77012
713-921-0235

T & M Plating Service
N3503 Highway 55
Chilton, WI 53014
920-439-2099 or 920-464-0154

Tri-City Plating Co.
218 E. Mill St.
Elizabethton, TN 37643
800-251-7536 or 423-542-1691
www.tricityplating.com

Vickerman Chrome
211 South McKinley St.
South Beloit, IL 61080
815-389-4700
www.vickermanschrome.com

Plastic Chrome (Metalizing)
Auto Instruments
2125 Virginia Ave.
Collinsville, VA 24078
877-450-0110
www.autoinstruments.com

Chrome-Tech USA
2314 Ravenswood Rd.
Madison, WI 53711
608-274-9811
www.chromtechusa.com

CV Vacuum Platers (Canada)
Unit No. 3
7160 Beatty Dr.
Mission, B.C. Canada V2V6B4
877-763-2323
www.cvvacuumplaters.com

CV Vacuum Platers (U.S.)
446 Harris St.
Sumas, WA 98295
604-820-9571
www.cvvacuumplaters.com

M&M Metalizing Sales
16478 Beach Blvd. No. 393
Westminster, CA 92683
714-822-6086
www.mmmetalizing.com

Mueller Corporation
530 Spring St.
East Bridgewater, MA 02333
508-583-2800
www.muellercorp.com

Plastic Resin Parts
Indian Bonnet
Chris Daniel
Mooresville, NC
cdaniel677@aol.com

Pot Metal Repair
Allied Technical Services
6239 Airport Way South
Seattle, WA 98108
206-763-3316
http://secruity-one.com/lesd/allied

Pot Metal Restorations
4794-C Woodlane Circle
Tallahassee, FL 32303
850-562-0538
www.customcoatings.net

Quality Pot Metal Works
2810 Parkway St. No. 5
Lakeland, FL 33811
863-640-0079

Powder Coating
House of Powder
Route 71 & 1st
Standard, IL 61363
815-339-2648
www.houseofpowder.com

Spence Industries, Inc.
1505 Cornell Rd.
Green Bay, WI 54313
920-662-0720

Woodwork/Woodgraining
R. L. Bailey
27902 45th Ave. S.
Auburn, WA 98001
253-854-5247
www.rbaileyrestoration.com

Classic Wood
Nampa, ID
208-467-2988

Classic Woodgraining
2640 Fairfield Pike
Springfield, OH 45502
866-472-4648
www.classicwoodgraining.com

Michael Couture
6415 N. 1060 West
Orland, IN 46776
260-829-1283

Custom Graining
5321 Erron Hill Rd.
Locke, NY 13092
315-729-5060
www.customgraining.com

Grad Davis
Washington
206-463-6110

Bill Gratkowski
515 N. Petroleum St.
Titusville, PA 16354
814-827-1782

C.D. Hall
1351 Locust Ave.
Long Beach, CA 90813
562-714-9118

KAT Performance Coatings
21838 Moens Rd.
Atkinson, IL 61235
309-936-1323
www.katcoatings.com

Ron Lawless
California
626-797-0266

Lokays Woodgraining
Florida
727-375-1797

Madera Concepts
55-B Depot Rd.
Goleta, GA 93117
800-800-1579
www.maderaconcepts.com

Main Street Custom Finishing
PO Box 945
www.mainstreetcustomfinishing.com

Lauren Matley
3205 SE 153rd Ave.
Vancouver, WA 98683
253-350-3604

Nichols Automotive Woodworking
Michigan
231-342-2090 or 231-922-9648

MAT Fabrication LLC
8124 Secura Way
Santa Fe Springs, CA 90670
562-693-6700
www.matfabrication.com

William Rau Automtive Woodwork
2027 Pontius Ave.
West Los Angeles, CA 90025
310-445-1128
www.rau-autowood.com

Royal Coach Works
2156 Lanceford Ln.
Lilburn, GA 30047
404-414-4952

Vintage Woodgraining, Inc.
1436 B. Patton Ave.
Asheville, NC 28806
828-254-0755
www.vintagewoodgraining.com

Vintage Woodworks
315 Depot Street
Iola, WI 54945
715-445-3791

Wood Doctor
5511 Silver Lake Dr.
West Bend, WI 53095
262-338-1033

Woodgrain 4 Wagons
4162 Levelside
Lakewood, CA 90712
562-425-6009
www.woodgrain4wagon.com

Woodgrain by Estes
2001 Charles St.
Lafayette, IN 47904
765-490-5634

Woodgrainings
Elk Grove, CA
916-683-2172
www.woodgrainings.com

Wire Wheel Repair
Dayton Wire Wheel
115 Compark Rd
Dayton, OH 45459
888-559-2880 or 937-438-0100
www.daytonwirewheel.com

CLASSES/CLUBS/MEDIA
Classes
Covell Creative Metalworking
106 Airport Blvd. No. 105
Freedom, CA 95019
800-747-4631 or 831-768-0705
www.covell.biz

Clubs
Fondy Vintage Auto
PO Box 131
Fond du Lac, WI 54936
(www.fondyvintageautoclub.com),

Metal Shapers
www.MetalShapers.org

Metal Meet
www.MetalMeet.com.

Media
Auto Trim & Restyling News
3520 Challenger St.
Torrance, CA 90503-1640
310-533-2400
www.atrn.com

Body Shop Business
3550 Embassy Parkway
Akron, OH 44333-8318
330-670-1234
www.bodyshopbusiness.com

Parts & People
450 Lincoln St.
Ste 110
Denver, CO 80203
303-765-4664
www.partsandpeople.com

Motorbooks International (MBI)
400 First Ave, North
Suite 300 Minneapolis, MN 55401
www.motorbooks.com

Old Cars Guide to Auto Restoration
Standard Catalog of Auto Restoration
700 E. State St.
Iola, WI 54990
715-445-2214
www.oldcarsweekly.com

Index

The Best Tools for the Job.

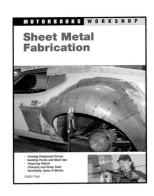

MOTORBOOKS WORKSHOP

Sheet Metal Fabrication

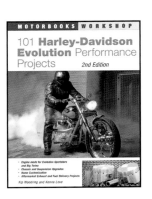

MOTORBOOKS WORKSHOP

101 Harley-Davidson Evolution Performance Projects 2nd Edition

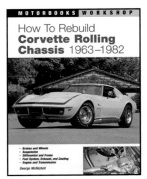

MOTORBOOKS WORKSHOP

How To Rebuild **Corvette Rolling Chassis** 1963–1982

MOTORBOOKS WORKSH

How to **Paint Your Car**

Other Great Books in this Series